DON'T SHOOT THE DOG!
THE NEW ART OF TEACHING AND TRAINING

"This delightful, clear, and utterly helpful book is for anyone who wants to understand or change the behavior of an animal—whether the animal in question is a sloppy spouse, a barking dog, a nosy neighbor, a lazy teenager, a whiny child, a hostile cat, or you and your own bad habits. Pryor explains why punishment—the 'take *take!*' style of trying to get people to change—so often fails, and she describes the specific methods that *do* work. This book will do more for human relations than all the well-meaning but vague pep talks to love thy neighbor, or improve thyself, for Pryor shows how to move from *intention* to *results*."

—Carol Tavris, Ph.D., author of *Anger*

"Another winner by Karen Pryor. A remarkable blend of the serious and humorous that translates behavioral training into everyday terms that are easy to understand and practice. If we would follow her recommendations in day-to-day life, there would be more productive kids, happier families and, best of all, a lot more fun in living."

—Betty Ann Countryman, Chairwoman of the Board of Directors, La Leche League International

"A wealth of relevant anecdotes . . . Pryor's treatment of 10 situations by each of eight methods is a perfect illustration of behavioral modification."

Weekly

"Dolphin trainer Karen Pryor offers behavioral training in . . . equally useful for shaping your cat's behavior or your dog, or getting rid of your own bad habits. . . . A fascinating, genuinely empowering book. Highly recommended."

—Tom Ferguson, *Medical Self-Care*

Don't Shoot the Dog!

The New Art of Teaching and Training

Karen Pryor

BANTAM BOOKS

NEW YORK · TORONTO · LONDON · SYDNEY · AUCKLAND

DON'T SHOOT THE DOG!

*A Bantam Book / published by arrangement with
Simon & Schuster*

PUBLISHING HISTORY

Bantam edition / September 1985

ISBN 0-553-25388-3

Published simultaneously in the United States and Canada

PRINTED IN THE UNITED STATES OF AMERICA

O   11   10

To my mother, *Sally Ondeck*
my stepmother, *Ricky Wylie*
and
Winifred Sturley,
my teacher and friend

Contents

In which we learn of the ferocity of Wall Street lawyers; of how to—and how not to—buy presents and give compliments; of a grumpy gorilla, a grudging panda, and a truculent teenager (the author); of gambling, pencil chewing, falling in love with heels, and other bad habits; of how to reform a scolding teacher or a crabby boss without their knowing what you've done; and more.

How to conduct an opera; how to putt; how to handle a bad report card. Parlor games for trainers. Notes on killer whales, Nim Chimpsky, Zen, Gregory Bateson, the Brearley School, why cats get stuck in trees, and how to train a chicken.

Orders, commands, requests, signals, cues, and words to the wise; what works and what doesn't. What discipline isn't. Who gets obeyed and why. How to stop yelling at your kids. Dancing, drill teams, music, martial arts, and other recreational uses of stimulus control.

Foreword

This book is about how to train anyone—human or animal, young or old, oneself or others—to do anything that can and should be done. How to get the cat off the kitchen table or your grandmother to stop nagging you. How to affect behavior in your pets, your kids, your boss, your friends. How to improve your tennis stroke, your golf game, your math skills, your memory. All by using the principles of training with reinforcement.

These principles are laws, like the laws of physics. They underlie all learning-teaching situations as surely as the law of gravity underlies the falling of an apple. Whenever we attempt to change behavior, in ourselves or in others, we are using these laws, whether we know it or not.

Usually we are using them inappropriately. We threaten, we argue, we coerce, we deprive. We pounce on others when things go wrong and pass up the chance to praise them when things go right. We are harsh and impatient with our children, with each other, with ourselves even; and we feel guilty over that harshness. We know that with better methods we could accomplish our ends faster, and without causing distress, but we can't conceive of those methods. We are just not attuned to the ways in which modern trainers take advantage of the laws of positive reinforcement.

Whatever the training task, whether keeping a four-year-old quiet in public, housebreaking a puppy, coaching a team, or memorizing a poem, it will go faster, and better, and be more fun, if you know how to use positive reinforcement.

The laws of reinforcement are simple; you can put the whole business on a blackboard in ten minutes and learn it in an hour. Applying these laws is more of a challenge; training by reinforcement is like a game, a game dependent upon quick thinking.

Anyone can be a trainer; some people are good at it from the very start. You do not need special qualities of patience, or a forceful personality, or a way with animals or children, or what circus trainer Frank Buck used to call the power of the human eye. You just need to know what you're doing.

There have always been people with an intuitive understanding of how to apply the laws of training. We call them gifted teachers, brilliant commanding officers, winning coaches, genius animal trainers. I've observed some theater directors and many symphony conductors who are wonderfully skilled at using reinforcement. These gifted trainers don't need a book to be able to take advantage of the laws that affect training. For the rest of us, however, those of us muddling along with an uncontrolled pet or at cross-purposes with a child or co-worker, a knowledge of how reinforcement really works can be a godsend.

Reinforcement training is not a system of rewards and punishments—by and large modern trainers don't even use those words. Rewards and punishments usually occur after an act is completed; often, as in criminal justice, long afterward. They may or may not affect behavior in the future. They certainly can't affect behavior that has already taken place. Reinforcement—whether "positive," something to be sought after, like a smile or a pat, or "negative," something to be avoided, like a tug on a leash or a frown—occurs while the behavior the trainer wishes o affect is going on. Correctly timed, reinforcement training works: It changes the behavior.

I first learned about training with positive reinforcement in Hawaii, where in 1963 I signed on as head dolphin trainer at an oceanarium, Sea Life Park. I had trained dogs and horses by traditional methods, but dolphins were a different proposition; you cannot use a leash or a bridle or even your fist on an animal that just swims away. Positive reinforcement—primarily a bucket of fish—was the only tool we had.

A psychologist outlined for me the principles of training by reinforcement. The art of applying those principles I learned from working with the dolphins. Schooled as a biologist, and with a lifelong interest in animal behavior, I found myself fascinated, not so much with the dolphins as with what could be communicated between us—from me to the animal *and* from the animal to me—during this kind of training. I applied what I'd learned from dolphin training to the training of other animals. And I began to notice some applications of the system creeping into my daily life. For example, I stopped yelling at my kids, because I was noticing that yelling didn't work. Watching for behavior I liked, and reinforcing it when it occurred, worked a lot better and kept the peace too.

There is a solid body of scientific theory underlying the lessons I learned from dolphin training. We shall go considerably beyond theory in this book, since as far as I know, the rules for *applying* these theories are largely undescribed by science and in my opinion often misapplied by scientists. But the fundamental laws are well established and must be taken into account when training.

This body of theory is variously known as behavior modification, reinforcement theory, operant conditioning, behaviorism, behavioral psychology, and so on: the branch of psychology largely credited to Harvard professor B. F. Skinner.

I know of no other modern body of scientific information that has been so vilified, misunderstood, misinterpreted, overinterpreted, and misused. The very name of Skinner arouses ire in those who champion "free will" as a characteristic that separates man from beast. To people schooled in the humanistic tradition, the manipulation of human behavior by some sort of conscious technique seems incorrigibly wicked, in spite of the obvious fact that we all go around trying to manipulate one another's behavior all the time, by whatever means come to hand.

While humanists have been attacking behaviorism and Skinner himself with a fervor that used to be reserved for religious heresies, behaviorism has swelled into a huge branch of psychology, with university departments, clinical practitioners, professional journals, international congresses, graduate-studies programs, doctrines, schisms, and masses and masses of literature.

And there have been benefits. Some disorders—autism, for example—seem to respond to shaping and reinforcement as to no other treatment. Many individual therapists have been extremely successful in solving the emotional problems of patients by using behavioral techniques. The effectiveness, at least in some circumstances, of simply altering behavior rather than delving into the origins of the behavior has contributed to the rise of family therapy, in which every family member's behavior is looked at, not just the behavior of the one who seems most obviously in distress. This makes eminent good sense.

Teaching machines and programmed textbooks derived from Skinnerian theory were early attempts to shape learning step by step and to reinforce the student for correct responses. These early mechanisms were clumsy but led directly to CAI, Computer-Assisted Instruction, which is great fun because of the amusing nature of the reinforcements (fireworks, dancing robots) and highly effective because of the computer's perfect timing. Reinforcement programs using tokens or chits that can be accumulated and traded for candy, cigarettes, or privileges have been established in mental hospitals and other institutions. Self-training programs for weight control and other habit changes abound. And biofeedback is an interesting application of reinforcement to training of physiological responses.

Academicians have studied the most minute aspects of conditioning. One finding shows, for example, that if you make a chart to keep track of your progress in some self-training program, you will be more likely to maintain new habits if you solidly fill in a little square every day on the chart, rather than just putting a check mark in the square.

This absorption with detail has valid psychological purposes, but I have not been able to find much good *training* in it. Training is a loop, a two-way communication in which an event at one end of the loop changes events at the other, exactly like a cybernetic feedback system; yet many psychologists treat their work as something they do to a subject, not with the subject. To a real trainer, the idiosyncratic and unexpected responses any subject can give are the most interesting and potentially the most fruitful events in the training process; yet almost all experimental work is designed to ignore or minimize individualistic responses. Devising methods for what Skinner named "shaping," the progressive changing of behavior, and carrying out those methods, is a creative process. Yet the psychological literature abounds with shaping programs that are so unimaginative, not to say ham-handed, that they constitute in my opinion cruel and unusual punishment. Take, for example, in one recent journal, a treatment for bed-wetting that involved not only putting "wetness" sensors in the child's bed but having the therapist spend the night with the child! The authors had the grace to say apologetically that it was rather expensive for the family. How about the expense to the child's psyche? This kind of "behavioral" solution is like trying to kill flies with a shovel.

Before going further, I must apologize to any professional behaviorists who are annoyed at my cavalier uses of the vocabulary of reinforcement theory. Skinner's vocabulary has an elegant specificity—*operant* conditioning, denoting that the subject is the "operator," as it were, not just a passive participant; *successive* approximation, suggesting the stair-step nature of the shaping procedure. In teaching training, however, I find that people balk at this unfamiliar verbiage; to get it across you would have to teach two things: the work and the proper way to converse about it. Meanwhile, in spreading from university to university, the Skinnerian vocabulary itself has undergone some modification; what some call a conditioned stimulus others call a discriminative stimulus, and still others a slangy "S_{Δ}." And hairsplitting redefinitions have proliferated. So I have sacrificed technical precision in favor of a vocabulary I think people can understand.

Schopenhauer once said that every original idea is first ridiculed, then vigorously attacked, and finally taken for granted. As far as I can see, reinforcement theory has been no exception. Skinner was widely ridiculed years ago for demonstrating shaping by developing a pair of Ping-Pong-playing pigeons. The warm, comfortable, self-cleansing, entertainment-providing crib he built for his infant daughters was derided as an inhumane "baby box," immoral and heretical. Rumors still go around that his daughters went mad, when in fact both of them are successful professional women and quite delightful people. Finally, nowadays many educated people treat reinforcement theory as if it were something not terribly important that they have known and understood all along. In fact most people *don't* understand it, or they would not behave so badly to the people around them.

In the years since my dolphin-training experiences, I have lectured and written about the laws of reinforcement in academic and professional circles as well as for the general public. I've taught this kind of training to high school, college, and graduate students, to housewives and zookeepers, to family and friends. I have watched and studied all kinds of other trainers, from cowboys to coaches, and I've noticed that the principles of reinforcement training are gradually seeping into our general awareness. Hollywood animal trainers call the use of positive reinforcement "affection training" and are using these techniques to accomplish behaviors impossible to obtain by force, such as the Merrill Lynch TV commercial of a bull strolling calmly through a china shop. Many Olympic coaches nowadays use positive reinforcement and shaping, instead of relying on old-fashioned browbeating, and have achieved notable improvements in performance.

Nowhere, however, have I found the rules of reinforcement theory written down so that they could be of use in immediate practical situations. So here they are, explained in this book as I understand them and as I see them used and misused in real life.

Reinforcement training does not solve all problems—it will not fatten your bank account, it cannot save a bad marriage, and it will not overhaul serious personality disorders. Some situations, such as a crying baby, are not training problems and require other kinds of solutions. Some behaviors, in animals and people, have genetic components that may be difficult or impossible to modify by training. Some problems are not worth the training time. But with many of life's challenges, tasks, and annoyances, correct use of reinforcement can help.

Practicing the use of positive reinforcement in one situation may induce you to apply it in others. As a dolphin researcher whom I worked with sourly put it, "Nobody should be allowed to have a baby until they have first been required to train a chicken," meaning that the experience of getting results with a chicken, an organism that cannot be trained by force, should make it clear that you don't need aggression to get results with a baby.

I have noticed that most dolphin trainers, who must develop the skills of positive reinforcement in their daily work, have strikingly pleasant and agreeable children. This book will not guarantee you agreeable children. In fact, it promises no specific results or skills. What it will give you is the fundamental principles underlying all training, and some guidelines on how to apply these principles creatively in varying situations. It will give you, in other words, the "art" of training. It may enable you to clear up annoyances that have been bothering you for years, or to make advances in areas where you have been stymied. It will certainly, if you wish, enable you to train a chicken.

There seems to be a natural order to reinforcement theory: These chapters come in the sequence in which training events, from simple to complex, really take place, and this is also the sequence in which people seem to learn most easily to be real trainers. The organization of this book is progressive in order to develop a comprehensive understanding of training through positive reinforcement. Its applications, however, are meant to be practical. Throughout the book's five chapters real-life situations are offered as illustration. Specific methods should be treated as suggestions or inspirations, rather than as definitive solutions.

Don't Shoot
the Dog!

1

Reinforcement: Better than Rewards

What Is Positive Reinforcement?

Positive reinforcement is anything which, occurring in conjunction with an act, tends to increase the probability that the act will occur again.

Memorize that statement. It is the secret of good training.

There are two kinds of reinforcement: positive and negative. A positive reinforcement is something the subject wants, such as food, petting, or praise. A negative reinforcement is something the subject wants to avoid—a blow, a frown, an unpleasant sound (the warning buzzer in cars if you don't fasten your seat belt is a negative reinforcement).

Behavior that is already occurring, no matter how sporadically, can always be intensified with positive reinforcement. If you call a puppy, and it comes, and you pet it, the pup's coming when called will become more and more reliable even without any other training. Suppose you want someone to telephone you—your offspring, your parent, your lover. If he or she doesn't call, there isn't much you can do about it. A major point in training with reinforcement is that you can't reinforce behavior that is not occurring. If, on the other hand, you are always delighted when your loved ones do call, so that the behavior is positively reinforced, the likelihood is that the incidence of their calling will probably increase. (Of course, if you apply negative reinforcement—"Why haven't you called, why do I have to call you, you never call me," and so on, remarks likely to annoy—you are setting up a situation in which the caller avoids such annoyance by not calling you; in fact, you are training them not to call.)

Simply offering positive reinforcement for a behavior is the most rudimentary part of reinforcement training. In the scientific literature, you can find psychologists saying, "Behavioral methods were used," or, "The problem was solved by a behavioral approach." All this means, usually, is that they switched to positive reinforcement from whatever other method they were using. It doesn't imply that they used the whole bag of tricks described in this book; they may not even be aware of them.

Yet switching to positive reinforcement is often all that is necessary. It is by far the most effective way to help the bed-wetter, for example: private praise and a hug for dry sheets in the morning, when they do occur.

Positive reinforcement can even work on yourself. At a Shakespeare study group I once belonged to I met a Wall Street lawyer in his late forties who was an avid squash player. The man had overheard me chatting about training, and on his way out the door afterward he remarked that he thought he would try positive reinforcement on his squash game. Instead of cursing his errors, as was his habit, he would try praising his good shots.

Two weeks later I ran into him again. "How's the squash game?" I asked. A look of wonder and joy crossed his face, an expression not frequently seen on Wall Street lawyers.

"At first I felt like a damned fool," he told me, "saying 'Way to go, Pete, attaboy,' for every good shot. Hell, when I was practicing alone, I even patted myself on the back. And then my game started to get better. I'm four rungs higher on the club ladder than I've ever been. I'm whipping people I could hardly take a point from before. And I'm having more fun. Since I'm not yelling at myself all the time, I don't finish a game feeling angry and disappointed. If I made a bad shot, never mind, good ones will come along. And I find I really enjoy it when the other guy makes a mistake, gets mad, throws his racquet—I know it won't help *his* game, and I just smile. . . ."

What a fiendish opponent. And just from switching to positive reinforcement.

Reinforcements are relative, not absolute. Rain is a positive reinforcement to ducks, a negative reinforcement to cats, and a matter of indifference, at least in mild weather, to cows. Food is not a positive reinforcement if you're full. Smiles and praise may be useless as reinforcement if the subject is trying to get you mad. In order to be reinforcing, the item chosen must be something the subject wants.

It is useful to have a variety of reinforcements for any training situation. At the Sea World oceanariums, killer whales are reinforced in many ways, with fish (their food), with stroking and scratching on different parts of the body, with social attention, toys, and so on. Whole shows are run in which the animals never know which behavior will be reinforced next or what the reinforcement will be; the "surprises" are so interesting for the animals that the shows can be run almost entirely without the standard fish reinforcements; the animals get their food at the end of the day. The necessity of switching constantly from one reinforcement to another is challenging and interesting for the trainers, too.

Positive reinforcement is good for human relationships. It is the basis of the art of giving presents: guessing at something that will be definitely reinforcing (guessing *right* is reinforcing for the giver, too). In our culture, present giving is often left to women. I even know of one family in which the mother buys all the Christmas presents to and from everyone. It causes amusement on Christmas morning, brothers and sisters saying, "Let's see, this is from Anne to Billy," when everyone knows Anne had nothing to do with it. But it does not sharpen the children's skills at selecting ways to reinforce other people.

In our culture a man who has become observant about positive reinforcement has a great advantage over other men. As a mother, I made sure that my sons learned how to give presents. Once, for example, when they were quite young, seven and five, I took them to a rather fancy store and had them select two dresses, one each, for their even younger sister. They enjoyed lolling about in the plush chairs, approving or disapproving of each dress as she modeled it, as much as any millionaire ever enjoyed helping a girlfriend pick out a mink coat. Their little sister enjoyed it too. And so, thanks to this and similar exercises, the lesson was learned: how to take a real interest in what *other* people want; how to enjoy finding effective positive reinforcements for the people you love.

Negative Reinforcement

Psychologists wrangle over the definition of negative reinforcement. For our purposes, a negative reinforcement is something a subject will work to avoid. Negative reinforcements may range from the mildest of aversive stimuli—a barely perceptible draft from an air conditioner that nevertheless makes you move to another table in a restaurant—to all kinds of extremes, such as electric shock.

Negative reinforcement is not punishment. Punishment comes after the behavior it is meant to affect. Thus you can't avoid receiving a punishment by changing your mind, or your actions, since the misbehavior has already happened. A boy being spanked for a bad report card may or may not get better report cards in the future, but he surely can't change the one he has just brought home. Negative reinforcement, on the other hand, may be halted or avoided by changing behavior right now. Suppose that while sitting in my aunt's living room I happen to put my feet on the coffee table. My aunt raises a disapproving eyebrow. I put my feet on the floor again. Her face relaxes. I feel relieved. And because I was able to halt the aversive stimulus, the behavior that occurred has been reinforced. I've learned something: Keep your feet off the furniture at Auntie's house.

Behavior can be trained entirely by negative reinforcement, as is the case with much traditional animal training: The horse learns to turn left when the left rein is pulled because of the annoying pressure that ceases when the turn is made; the lion backs onto a pedestal to avoid the intrusive whip or chair held near its face.

In general, "reinforcement" in this book refers to positive reinforcement; if I want to discuss negative reinforcement I shall say so specifically. By and large both kinds of reinforcements follow the same rules in application. For example, an error in timing will get you no results (or bad results) just as surely with one kind of reinforcement as with the other.

Timing of Reinforcement

As already stated, a reinforcement must occur in conjunction with the act it is meant to modify. A reinforcement is information. It tells the subject *exactly* what it is you like. When a subject is trying to learn, the informational content of a reinforcement becomes even more important than the reinforcement itself. In coaching athletes, or training dancers, it is the instructor's shouted "Yes!" or "Good!," marking a movement as it occurs, that truly gives the needed information—not the debriefing later in the dressing room.

Laggardly reinforcement is the beginning trainer's biggest problem. The dog sits, but by the time the owner says "Good dog," the dog is standing again. What does the animal think it got the "Good dog" for? Standing up. Whenever you find yourself having difficulties in a training situation, the first question to ask yourself is whether you are reinforcing too late. If you are working with an animal and are caught up in the thick of the action, it sometimes helps to have someone else watch for late reinforcements.

We are always reinforcing one another too late. "Gee, honey, you looked great last night" is quite different from the same comment said at the moment. The delayed reinforcement may even have deleterious effect ("What's the matter, don't I look great now?"). We have a touching trust in the powers of words to cover our lapses in timing.

Reinforcing too early is also ineffective. At the Bronx Zoo the keepers were having trouble with a gorilla. They needed to get it into its outdoor pen in order to clean the indoor cage, but it had taken to sitting in the doorway, where with its enormous strength it could prevent the sliding door from being closed. When the keepers put food outside, or waved bananas enticingly, the gorilla either ignored them or snatched the food and ran back to its door before it could be shut. A trainer on the zoo staff was asked to look at the problem. He pointed out that banana waving and the tossing in of food were attempts to reinforce behavior that hadn't occurred yet. The name for this is bribery. The solution was to ignore the gorilla when it sat in the door, but to reinforce it with food whenever it did happen to go out by itself. Problem solved.

Sometimes, I think, we reinforce children too soon under the misimpression that we are encouraging them ("Atta girl, that's the way, you almost got it right"). What we may be doing is reinforcing trying. There is a difference between trying to do something and doing it. Wails of "I can't" may sometimes be a fact, but they may also be symptoms of being reinforced too often merely for trying. In general, reinforcing behavior that hasn't occurred yet— with gifts, promises, compliments, or whatever—does not reinforce that behavior in the slightest. What it does reinforce is whatever was occurring at the time: soliciting reinforcement, most likely.

Timing is equally important when training with nega-
ve reinforcement. The horse learns to turn left when the
ft rein is pulled, but only if the pulling stops when it
oes turn. The cessation is the reinforcement. You get on
 horse, kick it in the sides, and it moves forward; you
hould then stop kicking (unless you want it to move
ster). Beginning riders often thump away constantly,
s if the kicking were some kind of gasoline necessary
) keep the horse moving. The kicking does not stop,
o it contains no information for the horse. Thus are
eveloped the iron-sided horses in riding academies that
nove at a snail's pace no matter how often they are
icked.

The same applies to people getting nagged and scolded
y parents, bosses, or teachers. If the negative reinforcement doesn't cease the instant the desired results are
chieved, it is not reinforcement nor is it information. It
ecomes, both literally and in terms of information theory,
noise."

Watching football and baseball on TV I am often
truck by the beautifully timed reinforcements the players
eceive again and again. As a touchdown is made, as the
unner crosses home plate, the roar of the crowd signals
nalloyed approval; and the instant a score is made or a
;ame is won, just watch the frenzied exchange of mutual
einforcements among the players. It is quite different for
ctors, especially movie actors. Even on stage, the ap-
lause comes after the job is done. For movie actors,
xcept for occasional response from a director or camera
perator or grip, there is no timely reinforcement; fan
etters and good reviews, arriving weeks or months later,
re pallid compared with all of Yankee Stadium going
erserk at the moment of success. No wonder some stars
ften exhibit a seemingly neurotic craving for adulation
nd thrills; the work can be peculiarly unsatisfying be-
ause the reinforcements, however splendid, are always
late."

Size of Reinforcement

Beginning trainers who use food reinforcement with animals are often confused as to how big each reinforcement should be. The answer is as small as you can get away with. The smaller the reinforcement, the more quickly the animal eats it. Not only does this cut down on waiting time, it also allows for more reinforcements per session, before the animal becomes satiated. In 1979 I was hired as a consultant by the National Zoological Park in Washington, D.C., to teach positive reinforcement techniques to a group of zoo employees. One of the keepers in my training class complained that her training of the panda had been proceeding too slowly. I thought this odd because intuitively I felt that pandas—big, greedy, active animals—should be easy to train with a reinforcement of food. I watched a session and found that while the keeper was gradually succeeding in shaping a body movement, she was giving the panda a whole carrot for each reinforcement. The panda took its own sweet time eating each carrot, so that in fifteen minutes of valuable keeper time it had earned only three reinforcements (and was incidentally getting tired of carrots). A single slice of carrot per reinforcement would have been better.

In general, a reinforcement that constitutes one small mouthful for that animal is enough to keep it interested—a grain or two of corn for a chicken, a quarter-inch cube of meat for a cat, half an apple for an elephant. With an especially preferred food you can go even smaller—a teaspoon of grain for a horse, for example. Keepers at the National Zoo have trained their polar bears to do many useful things, such as moving to another cage on command, with raisins.

A trainer's rule of thumb is that if you are going to have only one training session a day, you can count on the animal working well for about a quarter of its rations; you then give it the rest for free. If you can get in three or four sessions a day, you can divide the normal amount of food into about eighty reinforcements and give twenty or thirty in each session. Eighty reinforcements seems to be about the maximum for any subject's interest during any one day. (Perhaps that's why slide trays usually hold eighty slides; I know I always groan if a lecturer asks the projectionist for the second tray of slides.)·

The difficulty of the task also has some effect on the size of the reinforcement. At Sea Life Park we found it necessary to give each of our whales a large mackerel for their Olympic-effort, twenty-two-foot straight-up jump. They simply refused to do it for the usual reinforcement of two small smelt. For people, sometimes if not always, harder jobs get bigger rewards. And how we hate it when they don't, if we are the ones doing the hard job.

Jackpots

One extremely useful technique with food or any other reinforcement, for animals or people, is the jackpot. The jackpot is a reward that is much bigger, maybe ten times bigger, than the normal reinforcement, and one that comes as a surprise to the subject. At an ad agency where I once worked we had the usual office party at Christmas, as well as informal celebrations to signalize the completion of a big job or the signing of a new client. But the president was also in the habit of throwing one or two totally unexpected parties a year. Suddenly in midafternoon he would stride through all the offices, yelling for everyone to stop working. The switchboard was closed down, and in came a procession of caterers, musicians, bartenders, champagne, smoked salmon, the works: just for us and for no special reason. It was an unexpected jackpot for fifty people. It contributed vastly, I thought, to the company's high morale.

A jackpot may be used to mark a sudden breakthrough. In the case of one horse trainer I know, when a young horse executes a difficult maneuver for the first time, the man leaps from its back, snatches off saddle and bridle, and turns the horse loose in the ring—a jackpot of complete freedom, which often seems to make the new behavior stick in the animal's mind.

Paradoxically, a single jackpot may also be effective in improving the response of a recalcitrant, fearful, or resistant subject that is offering no desirable behavior at all. At Sea Life Park we were doing some U.S. Navy–funded research that involved reinforcing a dolphin for new responses, instead of old, previously trained behaviors. Our subject was a docile animal named Hou that rarely offered new responses. When she failed to get reinforced for what she did offer, she became inactive, and finally in one session she went twenty minutes offering no responses at all. The trainer finally tossed her two fish "for nothing." Visibly startled by this largesse, Hou became active again and soon made a movement that could be reinforced, leading to real progress in the next few sessions.

I had the same experience as that dolphin myself once. When I was fifteen my greatest pleasure in life was riding lessons. The stables where I rode sold tickets, ten lessons on a ticket: From my allowance I could afford one ticket a month. I was living with my father, Philip Wylie, and my stepmother, Ricky, at the time; and although they were very good to me, I had entered one of those adolescent periods in which one practices being as truculent and disagreeable as possible for days on end. One evening the Wylies, being loving and ingenious parents, told me that they were pretty tired of my behavior, and that what they had decided to do was reward me.

They then presented me with a brand-new, extra, free riding ticket. One of them had taken the trouble of going to the stables to buy it. Wow! An undeserved jackpot. As I recall, I shaped up on the spot, and Ricky Wylie confirmed that memory as I was writing this book many years later.

Why the unearned jackpot should have such abrupt and long-reaching effects I do not fully understand: Perhaps someone will do a Ph.D. dissertation on the matter someday and explain it to us. I do know that the extra riding ticket instantly relieved in me some strong feelings of oppression and resentment, and I suspect that's exactly how that dolphin felt, too.

Conditioned Reinforcers

It often happens, especially when training with food reinforcement, that there is absolutely no way you can get the reinforcement to the subject during the instant it is performing the behavior you wish to encourage. If I am training a dolphin to jump, I cannot possibly get a fish to it while it is in midair. If each jump is followed by a thrown fish (a delayed reward), eventually the animal will make the connection between jumping and eating and will jump more often. However, it has no way of knowing which aspect of the jump I liked. Was it the height? The arch? Perhaps the splashing reentry? Thus it would take many repetitions to identify to the animal the exact sort of jump I had in mind. To get around this problem we use conditioned reinforcers.

A conditioned reinforcer is some initially meaningless signal—a sound, a light, a motion—that is deliberately associated with the arrival of a reinforcement. Dolphin trainers have come to rely on the police whistle as a conditioned reinforcer; it is easily heard, even underwater, and it leaves one's hands free for signaling and fish throwing. With other animals I frequently use a cricket, the dime-store party toy that goes "click-click" when you press it, or a particular praise word, selected and reserved for the purpose of acting as a conditioned reinforcer: "Good dog," "Good pony." Schoolteachers often arrive at some such ritualized and carefully rationed word of commendation—"That's fine" or "Very good"—for which the children anxiously work and wait.

Conditioned reinforcers abound in our lives. We like to hear the phone ring or see a full mailbox, even if half our calls are no fun or most of our mail is junk mail, because we have had numerous occasions to learn to associate the ringing or the envelopes with good things. We like Christmas music and hate the smell of dentists' offices. We keep things around us—pictures, dishes, trophies—not because they are beautiful or useful but because they remind us of times when we were happy or of people we love. They are conditioned reinforcers.

Practical animal training that uses positive reinforcement should almost always begin with the establishment of a conditioned reinforcer. Before the start of any real training of behavior, while the subject is doing nothing in particular, you teach it to understand the significance of the conditioned reinforcer by pairing it with food, petting, or other real reinforcements. You can tell, incidentally, at least with animals, when the subject has come to recognize your signal for "Good!" It visibly startles on perceiving the conditioned reinforcer and begins seeking the real reinforcement. With the establishment of a conditioned reinforcer you have a real way of communicating exactly what you like in the animal's behavior. So you do not need to be Dr. Dolittle to talk to the animals; you can "say" an amazing amount with such trained reinforcement.

Conditioned reinforcers become immensely powerful. Because the information "You're right" is valuable in itself, one need not always follow with the primary reinforcer. In fact the use of food, or petting, or whatever can be rationed down to practically nothing, while the conditioned reinforcer continues to get excellent results. I have seen marine mammals work long past the point of satiety for conditioned reinforcers, and horses and dogs work for an hour or more with little or no primary reinforcement. People, of course, work endlessly for money, which is after all only a conditioned reinforcer, a token for the things it can buy—even, or perhaps especially, people who have already earned more money than they can actually spend, who have accordingly become addicted to the conditioned reinforcer.

One can make a conditioned reinforcer more powerful by pairing it with several primary reinforcements. The subject at that moment may not want food, say, but if the same reinforcing sound or word has also been associated deliberately with water, or some other needs or pleasures, it retains its usefulness and then some. My cats hear "Good girl!" when their supper dish is put down, when they are petted, when they are let in and out, and when they do little tricks and get treats for them. Consequently, I can use "Good girl!" to reinforce getting off the kitchen table, without having to follow up with an actual reinforcement. Probably the reason money is so reinforcing for us is that it can be paired with practically everything. It is an extremely generalized conditioned reinforcer.

Once you have established a conditioned reinforcer, you must be careful not to throw it around meaninglessly or you will dilute its force. The children who rode my Welsh ponies for me quickly learned to use "Good pony!" only when they wanted to reinforce behavior. If they just wanted to express affection, they could chat to the pony any way they liked, except in those words. One day a child who had just joined the group was seen petting a pony's face while saying "You're a good pony." Three of the others rounded on her instantly: "What are you telling him that for? He hasn't done anything!" Similarly one can and should lavish children (and spouses, parents, lovers, and friends) with love and attention, unrelated to any particular behavior; but one should reserve praise, specifically, as a conditioned reinforcer related to something real. There are plenty of such real events deserving praise, a reinforcement that is abundantly exchanged in happy families. False or meaningless praise, however, is soon resented, even by tiny children, and loses any power to reinforce.

One can also develop a conditioned negative reinforcer, which can be very useful. Children and some animals will often react immediately to a sharp, loud "No!" without pairing it with something else. It seems to be a primary, or unconditioned, negative reinforcer. But many

35

animals—cats, notoriously—ignore shouts or scolding. A friend of mine cured her cat of clawing the couch by establishing "no" as a conditioned negative reinforcer quite accidentally. One day in the kitchen she happened to drop a large brass tray, accidentally, right next to the cat, and she cried "No!" as the tray fell with a loud clatter. The cat was dreadfully startled and jumped into the air with all its fur on end. The next time the cat clawed the couch she exclaimed "No!" and the cat, looking horrified, desisted immediately; two or three repetitions of the now-conditioned word were enough to make it end the behavior permanently.

Schedules of Reinforcement

There is a popular misconception that if you start training a behavior by positive reinforcement you will have to keep on using positive reinforcement for the rest of the subject's natural life; if not, the behavior will disappear. This is untrue; constant reinforcement is needed just in the *learning* stages. You might praise a toddler repeatedly for using the toilet, but once the behavior has been learned, the matter takes care of itself. We give, or we should give, the beginner a lot of reinforcement—teaching a kid to ride a bicycle may involve a constant stream of "That's right, steady now, you got it, *good*!" However, you'd look pretty silly (and the child would think you were crazy) if you went on praising once the behavior had been acquired.

In order to maintain an already-learned behavior with some degree of reliability, it is not only not necessary to reinforce it every time; it is vital that you do *not* reinforce it on a regular basis but instead switch to using reinforcement only occasionally, and on a random or unpredictable basis.

This is what psychologists call a variable schedule of reinforcement. A variable schedule is *far more* effective in maintaining behavior than a constant, predictable schedule of reinforcement. One psychologist explained it to me his way: If you have a new car, one that has always started easily, and you get in one day and turn the key and it doesn't start, you may try a few more times, but soon you are going to decide something is wrong and go call the garage. Your key-turning behavior, in the absence of the expected, immediate reinforcement, quickly extinguishes, or dies out. If, on the other hand, you have an old clunker that almost never starts on the first try, and often takes forever to get going, you may try and try to start it for half an hour; your key-turning behavior is on a long, variable schedule, and is thereby strongly maintained.

If I were to give a dolphin a fish every time it jumped, very quickly the jump would become as minimal and perfunctory as the animal could get away with. If I then stopped giving fish, the dolphin would quickly stop jumping. However, once the animal had learned to jump for fish, if I were to reinforce now the first jump, then the third, and so on at random, the behavior would be much more strongly maintained; the unrewarded animal would actually jump more and more often, hoping to hit the lucky number, as it were, and the jumps might even increase in vigor. This in turn would allow me to selectively reinforce the more vigorous jumps, thus using my variable schedule to shape improved performance. But even some professional animal trainers fail to make good use of variable schedules of positive reinforcement; it seems to be a peculiarly difficult concept for many people to accept intellectually. We recognize that we don't need to go on punishing misbehavior if the misbehavior stops, but we don't see that it's not necessary or even desirable to reward correct behavior continuously. We are less sure of ourselves when aiming for disciplined response through positive reinforcement.

The power of the variable schedule is at the root of all gambling. If every time you put a nickel into a slot machine a dime were to come out, you would soon lose interest. Yes, you would be making money, but what a boring way to do it. People like to play slot machines precisely because there's no predicting whether nothing will come out, or a little money, or a lot of money, or *which* time the reinforcement will come (it might be the very first time). Why some people get addicted to gambling and others can take it or leave it is another matter, but for those who do get hooked, it's the variable schedule of reinforcement that does the hooking.

The longer the variable schedule, the more powerfully it maintains behavior. Long schedules work against you, however, if you are trying to eliminate a behavior. Unreinforced, any behavior will tend to die down by itself; but if it is reinforced from time to time, however sporadically—one cigarette, one drink, one giving in to the nagger or whiner, the behavior, instead of being extinguished, may actually be strongly maintained by a long, variable schedule. That is how the ex-smoker who sneaks an occasional cigarette can go back to being a heavy smoker in a day.

We have all seen people who inexplicably stick with spouses or lovers who mistreat them. Customarily we think of this as happening to a woman—she falls for someone who is harsh, inconsiderate, selfish, even cruel, and yet she loves him—but it happens to men, too. Everyone knows such people, who, if divorced or otherwise bereft of the nasty one, go right out and find someone else just like him or her.

Are these people, for deep psychological reasons, perpetual victims? Possibly. But may they not also be victims of long-duration variable schedules? If you get into a relationship with someone who is fascinating, charming, sexy, fun, and attentive, and then gradually the person becomes more disagreeable, even abusive, though still showing you the good side now and then, you will live for those increasingly rare moments when you are getting all that wonderful reinforcement: the fascinating, charming, sexy, and fun attentiveness. And paradoxically from a commonsense viewpoint, though obviously from the training viewpoint, the rarer and more unpredictable those moments become, the more powerful will be their effect as reinforcers, and the longer your basic behavior will be maintained. Furthermore, it is easy to see why someone once in this kind of relationship might seek it out again. A relationship with a normal person who is decent and friendly most of the time might seem to lack the kick of that rare, longed-for and thus doubly intense reinforcer.

Look at it from the manipulator's point of view: I can have her/him eating out of my hand, and doing whatever I want, for my comfort and convenience solely, as long as I give her/him what she/he wants . . . once in a while. That's one way pimps keep their whores in line. It's a powerful fix, all right, but once the victim appreciates that the intensity of the "charm" is at least partly due to the nature of the reinforcement schedule, he or she can usually walk quietly away from this kind of relationship and look for something else.

Exceptions to Variable Reinforcement

The one circumstance when one should not go to a variable schedule once the behavior has been learned is when the behavior involves solving some kind of puzzle or test. In advanced obedience training, dogs are asked to select from a group of miscellaneous objects the single object their owner had handled and scented. It is necessary to tell the dog each time that it has selected correctly, so it will know what to do next time. In discrimination tests—identifying the higher of two sounds, let us say—the subject must be reinforced for each correct response so that it continues to be informed as to what question it is being asked (a conditioned reinforcer will do, of course). When we play with crossword or jigsaw puzzles, we get reinforced for correct guesses because those are the only ones that "fit." In doing a jigsaw puzzle, if you could put several pieces in each hole you would not get the positive reinforcement for the right choice, which is necessary feedback in any kind of choice-trial situation.

Long-Duration Behaviors

In addition to variable schedules, one can also establish fixed schedules of reinforcement, in which the subject knows it must work for a predetermined length of time or accomplish a predetermined number of behaviors for each reinforcement. For example, I could arrange for a dolphin to jump six times in a row by reinforcing every sixth jump; soon I would be getting a routine series of six. The trouble with fixed schedules is that the early responses in the series are never reinforced, so they tend to dwindle down to some minimal effort. With the jumping dolphin, in due course all the jumps but the last one, the one that is actually reinforced, would get smaller. This dwindling effect of fixed schedules is probably a factor in many human tasks—factory assembly lines, for example. It is necessary to work for a certain length of time in order to get reinforced, but since the reinforcement is on a fixed schedule, regardless of quality of performance, the subject quite naturally is motivated to do the least amount of work possible to still stay in the game, and may perform especially poorly at the start of the work period. Payday on Friday is a fixed reinforcement leading directly to Blue Monday. With the dolphins, occasional random reinforcements for the first or second jump as well as the sixth will help maintain behavior. With people, various kinds of incentive bonuses or other reinforcements (awards, for example) tied directly to quality and quantity of production, and arriving out of synchrony with the usual reinforcement, can be effective.

Using either fixed or variable schedules, extremely long sequences of behavior can be trained. A baby chick can be induced to peck a button a hundred times or more for each grain of corn. For humans there are many examples of delayed gratification. One psychologist jokes that the longest schedule of unreinforced behavior in human existence is graduate school.

In extremely long schedules, there is sometimes a

point of no return. For the baby chick that point is meta-
bolic; when the chick expends more energy pecking than
it can get back from the grain of corn it receives, the
behavior tends to die down—the rewards of the job have
fallen so low that it simply isn't worth doing. This of
course often happens with people as well.

Another phenomenon occurs on very long schedules:
slow starts. The chick pecks away at a steady rate once it
gets started, because each peck brings it nearer to reinforcement, but researchers have noted that a chick tends
to "put off" starting for longer periods as the schedule of
reinforcement gets longer. This is called "delayed start of
long-duration behavior," and it's a very familiar aspect of
human life. On any long task, from doing the income taxes
to cleaning out the garage, one can think of endless reasons for not starting now. Writing, even sometimes just
the writing of a letter, is a long-duration behavior. Once it
gets started things usually roll along fairly well, but, oh!
it's so hard to make oneself sit down and begin. James
Thurber found it so difficult to start an article that he
sometimes fooled his wife (who was understandably anx-
ious for him to write articles since that was how the rent
got paid) by lying on a couch in his study all morning
reading a book in one hand while tapping the typewriter
keys at random with the other. The delayed-start phenomenon outweighed the prospect of eventual positive
reinforcement of money; and the sham typing at least
staved off the negative reinforcement of wifely reproaches.

One way to overcome the slow-start phenomenon is
to introduce some reinforcement just for getting started,
just as I sporadically reinforced my dolphins for the first or
second jump in a six-jump series. I have used this technique effectively in self-training. For some years I went to
graduate school one or two nights a week, a long business
involving three hours of class and an hour on the subway
each way. It was always a huge temptation, as five o'clock
rolled around, not to go. But then I found that if I broke
down the journey, the first part of the task, into five

steps—walking to the subway, catching the train, changing to the next train, getting the bus to the university, and finally, climbing the stairs to the classroom—and reinforced each of these initial behaviors by consuming a small square of chocolate, which I like but normally never eat, at the completion of each step, I was at least able to get myself out of the house, and in a few weeks was able to get all the way to class without either the chocolate or the internal struggle.

Superstitious Behavior: Accidental Reinforcements

Reinforcements occur all the time in real life, often by coincidence. A biologist studying hawks noticed that if a hawk caught a mouse under a particular bush, it would check out that bush every day for a week or so thereafter; the probability that it would fly over that particular spot had been strongly reinforced. Find a five-dollar bill in a trash basket, and I defy you to walk past that trash basket the next day without looking it over closely.

Accidental reinforcement was beneficial to the hawk; in fact animal behavior in general might be said to have evolved so as to enable each species to benefit from whatever reinforcements occur. However, many accidental reinforcements also happen with trivial benefits or none, and these can still have a strong effect on behavior. When the behavior is unrelated to the consequences but becomes fixed in the subject's mind as necessary for reinforcement, scientists call it superstitious behavior. An example is pencil chewing. If, while taking an exam, you happen to put your pencil in your mouth and just then the right answer or a good idea occurs to you, the reinforcement may affect the behavior; good ideas occur during pencil chewing, so pencil chewing is reinforced. When I was in college I didn't own a pencil that wasn't covered with teeth marks—on really tough exams I sometimes bit pencils right in two. I even felt sure that pencil chewing helped me to think; of course it didn't, it was just accidentally conditioned behavior.

The same goes for wearing a particular garment or going through a ritual when you are about to engage in a task. I have seen one baseball pitcher who goes through a nine-step chain of behavior every time he gets ready to pitch the ball: touch cap, touch ball to glove, push cap forward, wipe ear, push cap back, scuff foot, and so on. In a tight moment he may go through all nine steps twice, never varying the order. The sequence goes by quite fast—announcers never comment on it—and yet it is a very elaborate piece of superstitious behavior.

Superstitious behavior often crops up in training animals. The animal may be responding to criteria you had no intention of establishing but which were accidentally reinforced often enough to become conditioned. For example, the animal may think it has to be in a particular place or facing or sitting a certain way to earn reinforcement. When you want it to work in a new place or face another way, suddenly the behavior mysteriously breaks down, and figuring out why may take some doing. It is wise, therefore, once a behavior has been at least partially trained, to introduce variations in all the circumstances that do not matter to you, lest some accidental conditioning develop that might get in your way later.

Above all, watch out for the development of accidental patterns of timing. Both animals and people have a very clear sense of time intervals. I was once quite convinced that I had trained two porpoises to jump on command (a hand signal from me) until a visiting scientist with a stopwatch informed me that they were jumping every twenty-nine seconds. Sure enough, with or without my command, they jumped every twenty-nine seconds. *I* had become accidentally conditioned to give the command with great regularity, and they had picked up on that instead of on the information I thought they were using.

Many traditional animal trainers are absolutely riddled with superstitious thinking and behavior. I have had some tell me that dolphins prefer people to wear white, that you have to hit mules, that bears don't like women, and so on. And people trainers can be just as bad, believing you have to yell at fifth-graders, for example, or that punishment is needed to create respect. Such trainers are at the mercy of tradition; they have to train the same way every time because they can't separate the methods that are working from methods that are merely superstitious. This failing or confusion crops up in many professions— education, engineering, the military, and perhaps particularly in the medical profession. It is appalling how many things are done to patients not because they are curative but simply because that's the way it's always been done or that's what everyone does nowadays. Anyone who has ever been a patient in a hospital can think of half a dozen examples of unnecessary acts that amounted to nothing more than superstitious behavior.

Interestingly enough, superstitious behavior does not go away if you merely point out its ineffectiveness; strongly conditioned, it is accordingly strongly defended. Attack a doctor for his or her habitual use of a nonhelpful or even harmful treatment, and you will be attacked right back—in spades; as I'm sure that pitcher with the nine-step superstitious windup would resist fiercely anyone ordering him to play ball without, say, wearing the cap he touches four times in the sequence.

One way to get rid of superstitious behavior is just to become aware that it has no relation to reinforcement. My son Ted is a banker whose hobby is competitive fencing. He fits in practice bouts two or three times a week and often travels to tournaments on weekends. One day, facing a stiff competitor, he felt downcast because he had left his favorite blade at home. He lost the match. Then he realized that feeling downcast was probably far more damaging to his performance than the blade he used, and, in fact, that having a "favorite" blade was superstitious behavior.

Ted set out to eliminate every superstitious behavior he could identify related to fencing. He discovered many in his repertoire, from attachment to certain articles of clothing to inner convictions that his game might be affected by a bad night's sleep, an argument, or even by running out of fruit juice at a tournament. Systematically examining each of these circumstances, he eliminated his dependencies one by one as he recognized them as superstitious behavior. Consequently, he now enters each fray relaxed and confident, even if the previous hours have been a nightmare of missed trains, lost gear, and battles with taxi drivers, and even if he is fencing with a borrowed blade in a practice uniform with mismatched socks.

What Can You Do with Positive Reinforcement?

Here are some things people I know have done with positive reinforcement:

- Judy, a designer, took a weekly painting class at night at a nearby university to keep her hand in; most of the twenty other people in the class were also designers or commercial artists. The teacher assigned weekly homework, which many of the busy professionals did not bother to complete. The teacher habitually harangued the class for ten minutes or more over the poor showing of homework assignments. Tired of being scolded, Judy suggested he reinforce the ones who did bring in assignments instead of heckling those who didn't. He did so, reinforcing his pupils with public praise of each completed assignment. By the third week, the teacher not only had a happier class, he had raised the number of homeworkers from about a third of the class to nearly three-quarters.
- Shannon, a college student, visited the home of some friends and walked in on a scene. Four adults were trying, unsuccessfully and at some risk to themselves, to restrain the household German shepherd so the dog's

infected ear could be medicated. Shannon, not a dog lover particularly but a student of positive reinforcement, got some cheese from the refrigerator and in five minutes trained the dog to hold still while she medicated his ear single-handed.

- A young woman married a man who turned out to be very bossy and demanding. Worse yet, his father, who lived with them, was equally given to ordering his daughter-in-law about. It was the girl's mother who told me this story. On her first visit she was horrified at what her daughter was going through. "Don't worry, Mother," the daughter said. "Wait and see." The daughter formed a practice of responding minimally to commands and harsh remarks, while reinforcing with approval and affection any tendency by either man to be pleasant or thoughtful. In a year she had turned them into decent human beings. Now they greet her with smiles when she comes home and leap up—both of them—to help with the groceries.

- An urban eighth-grader liked to take her dog for walks on weekends in the country, but the dog often ran off too far and refused to come back when called, especially when it was time to go home. One weekend the girl started making a huge fuss over the dog—praise, patting, baby talk, hugs, the works—whenever, in running about, it came up to her unbidden. When it was time to go home, she called and the dog came gladly. The huge welcome apparently outweighed, as a reinforcement, the dog's usual prolongation of freedom. It never gave trouble on country walks again.

- A junior executive with a monster of a boss decided which parts of his job might be reinforcing to the boss— bringing papers to be signed, for example—and timed as many as possible to coincide with periods when the boss was not in a rage. The boss eased up and in due course actually started telling jokes.

- Some people develop very special reinforcements that others will go out of their way to earn. Annette, a suburban housewife whose children are grown, might be rather isolated were it not for her network of friends who phone weekly or even more often to share their news. These are not necessarily neighbors or relatives; many are busy professional women who live far away. I am one. Why do we all call Annette? If you have bad news—you've got the flu, or the IRS is going to audit you, or the baby-sitter moved to Cleveland—Annette gives sympathy and advice; but so would any friend. It is in the area of good news that Annette offers unusual reinforcement. Tell her the bank approved your loan, and she does more than say "That's great!" She points out exactly what you did to earn and deserve the good news. "You see?" Annette might respond. "Remember how hard you worked to get a good credit rating? Remember all the trouble you went to with the phone company, and getting an air-travel card? Now it pays off for you; you're recognized as a good businesswoman. But you had to make the right moves first, and you did. I'm really proud of you." Wow! That's more than approval, that is reinforcement—and for past efforts which at the time may have seemed to be merely tribulations. Annette takes good news out of the "good luck" category and turns it into reinforcement. That certainly reinforces one's inclination to call Annette.

Organized Reinforcement

Sales meetings, booster clubs, Dale Carnegie courses, Weight Watchers, in fact most organizations that teach self-improvement in groups, rely heavily on the effects of reinforcement by the group upon individuals. Applause, medals, awards ceremonies, and other forms of group recognition are powerful reinforcements, sometimes quite imaginatively used. One IBM sales manager, wishing to reinforce his sales team for a good year, hired a football stadium; threw a big party for the employees, senior executives, and all their families; and had his sales force run through the players' tunnel onto the field while their names were flashed on the scoreboard, to the cheers of all assembled.

Several years ago I went through Werner Erhard's "est" course, a program with overtones of hucksterism but which, from a training standpoint, I found to be an ingenious and often brilliant application of shaping and reinforcement. The program was called, rightly I think, the Training. The leader was called the Trainer. The shaping goal was improved self-awareness, and the principal reinforcement was not the Trainer's responses but the nonverbal behavior of the whole group.

To develop group behavior as a reinforcer, the 250 people in the group were told to applaud after every speaker, whether they felt like applauding or not. Thus from the beginning the shy were encouraged, the bold rewarded, and all contributions, whether insightful or inane, were acknowledged by the group.

At first the applause was dutiful and no more. Soon it became genuinely communicative—not of degrees of enjoyment, as in the theater, but of shades of feeling and meaning. For example: there was in my training class, as I expect there is in every est group, an argumentative man who frequently took issue with what the Trainer said. When this happened for the third or fourth time, the Trainer started arguing back. Now, it was apparent to all that from a logical standpoint, the argumentative man was perfectly correct. But as the argument wore on and on, no one else in the room cared who was right. All 249 of us just wished he'd shut up and sit down.

The rules of the game—shaping rules, really—did not permit us to protest or to tell him to shut up. But gradually, the massive silence of the group percolated into his awareness. We watched him realize that no one cared if he was right. Maybe being right was not the only game in town. Slowly he sputtered into silence and sat down. The group instantly erupted in a huge burst of applause, expressive of sympathy and understanding as well as of hearty relief—a very powerful positive reinforcement for the illumination the arguer had just received.

This kind of training occurrence, in which the important events are behavioral and thus nonverbal, is often maddeningly difficult to explain to an outsider. Erhard, like a Zen teacher, often resorts to aphorisms; in the case of the arguer described above, the est saying is "When you're right, that's what you get to be: right." That is, not necessarily loved, or anything else nice: just right. If I were to quote that aphorism at a party when somebody is being bombastic, another est graduate might laugh—and indeed, any good modern trainer might laugh—but most hearers might assume I was moronic or drunk. Good training insights do not necessarily lend themselves to verbal explanation.

Reinforcing Yourself

One of the most useful practical applications of reinforcement is reinforcing yourself. This is something we often neglect to do, partly because it doesn't occur to us, and partly because we tend to demand a lot more of ourselves than we would of others. As a minister I know put it, "Few of us have such low standards that it's easy to live up to them." As a result we often go for days at a time without letup, going from task to task to task unnoticed and unthanked even by ourselves. Quite aside from reinforcing oneself for some habit change or new skill, a certain amount of reinforcement is desirable just for surviving daily life; deprivation of reinforcement is one factor, I think, in states of anxiety and depression.

You can reinforce yourself in healthful ways—with an hour off, a walk, a talk with friends, or a good book; or in unhealthful ways—with cigarettes, whiskey, fattening food, drugs, late nights, and so on. I like performer Ruth Gordon's suggestion: "An actor has to have compliments. If I go long enough without getting a compliment, I compliment myself, and that's just as good because at least then I know it's sincere."

2
Shaping: Developing Super Performance Without Strain or Pain

What Is Shaping?

Reinforcing behavior which is already occurring, so that it occurs more often, is all very well, but how do trainers get their subjects to do things that would probably never occur by chance? How do you get a dog to turn back flips or a dolphin to jump through a hoop?

Dogs flipping, dolphins jumping through hoops, or people throwing basketballs through hoops, for that matter, are developed by shaping. Shaping consists of taking a very small tendency in the right direction and shifting it, one small step at a time, toward an ultimate goal. The laboratory jargon for the process is successive approximation.

Shaping is possible because the behavior of living things is variable. Whatever a creature does, it will do it with more vigor at some times than at others, in different directions, and so on. No matter how elaborate or difficult the ultimate behavior you wish to shape, you can always, by establishing a series of intermediate goals, find some behavior presently occurring to use as a first step. For example, suppose I decided to train a chicken to "dance." I might begin by watching the chicken moving around as chickens do and reinforcing it every time it happened to move to the left. Soon my first goal would be reached: the chicken would be moving to the left quite often—and, being variable, sometimes a little and sometimes a lot. Now I might selectively reinforce only the stronger movements to the left—turning a quarter circle, say. When these responses predominated, natural variability would again ensure that while some turns were less than a quarter circle, some would be more like half a circle. I could raise my criteria, set a new goal, and start selecting for half-circle turns or better. With the chicken shaped to make several full turns at high speed per reinforcement, I might consider that I'd reached my end goal, a dancing chicken.

We are all quite accustomed to shaping and being shaped. In an informal way much of child rearing is a shaping process. The training of any physical skill, from tennis to typing, consists largely of shaping. We are shaping or at least trying to shape any time we practice something, from a public speech to scales on the piano. We are also shaping when we try to change our own behavior—to quit smoking, say, or to be less shy, or to handle money better.

Whether we succeed or don't succeed in shaping a behavior, in ourselves or in others, ultimately depends *not* upon our shaping expertise but upon persistence. *New York Times* music critic Harold Schonberg wrote of a European conductor who was not really a good conductor but who made fabulous music by keeping his orchestra in rehearsal for each concert for a full year. Most of us can acquire at least some proficiency at almost anything, if we just put enough time into it.

But that's boring. Don't we always want to learn new skills—skiing, piano playing, whatever—as fast as possible? Of course we do, and that's where *good* shaping comes in. Further, don't we prefer to avoid or minimize repetition? Yes again. Of course, some physical skills require repetition, because muscles "learn" slowly and must be put through the motions repeatedly before the motions come easily. Even so, a well-planned shaping program can minimize the required drilling and can make every moment of practice count, thus speeding up progress tremendously. And finally, in sports, music, and other creative endeavors, you may want to develop not only reliable performance but as good a performance as you or the one you're training can possibly give. In that case, correct use of the laws governing shaping may be crucial.

Methods Versus Principles

There are two aspects to shaping: the methods—that is, the behaviors that are to be developed and the sequence of steps used to develop them—and the principles, or rules, governing how, when, and why those behaviors are reinforced.

Most trainers, most books about training, and most teachers of training are concerned almost entirely with method. "Place your hands on the golf club as in the drawing"; "Line up your rifle sights before you aim at the target"; "Never lean into the mountain"; "Beat the eggs with a wire whisk in a clockwise direction." This is fine. Such methods usually have been developed over many years, by many people, through trial and error, so they do work. It's really true that you'll sit on a horse more securely if you keep your heels down, or that your golf ball will go farther if you shape a good follow-through into your swing. If you are interested in learning a particular skill, I would strongly urge that you find out as much as possible about the established methods of accomplishing the behaviors which that skill involves, through books, teachers, or coaches and through watching or studying others.

On the other side of shaping, however, are the principles, the rules that control such matters as when to press on and when to let up; how to escalate your criteria most efficiently; what to do when you run into trouble; above all, perhaps, when to quit. These questions are generally left to the intuition and experience of trainers or coaches, or to chance or luck. Yet it is the successful application of such principles that makes the difference between an adequate teacher and a great one, and between shaping that is happy, fast, and successful and frustrating, slow, boring, and disagreeable. It's good shaping, not just good methods, that makes training effective.

The Ten Laws of Shaping

There are ten rules that govern shaping, as I see it. Some—the first four, at least—come straight from the psychology labs and have been demonstrated experimentally. Others have not even been the subject of formal study, so far as I know, but can be recognized as inherently valid laws by anyone who has done a lot of shaping: You always know (usually an instant too late) when you've broken one. I'll list the rules here, then discuss each one at some length:

1. Raise criteria in increments small enough so that the subject always has a realistic chance for reinforcement.
2. Train one thing at a time; don't try to shape for two criteria simultaneously.
3. Always put the current level of response onto a variable schedule of reinforcement before adding or raising criteria.
4. When introducing a new criterion, temporarily relax the old ones.
5. Stay ahead of your subject: Plan your shaping program completely so that if the subject makes sudden progress you are aware of what to reinforce next.
6. Don't change trainers in midstream; you can have several trainers per trainee but stick to one shaper per behavior.
7. If one shaping procedure is not eliciting progress, find another; there are as many ways to get behavior as there are trainers to think them up.

8. Don't interrupt a training session gratuitously; that constitutes a punishment.
9. If behavior deteriorates, "go back to kindergarten"; quickly review the whole shaping process with a series of easy reinforcements.
0. End each session on a high note, if possible, but in any case quit while you're ahead.

Discussion

. *Raise criteria in increments small enough so that the subject always has a realistic chance of reinforcement.*

In practice this means that when you increase demands or raise a criterion for reinforcement, you should do so within the range the subject is already achieving. If your horse clears two-foot jumps, sometimes with a foot to spare, you could start raising some jumps to two and a half feet. Raising them all to three feet would be asking for trouble: The animal is capable of this but is not offering it regularly yet. And raising the jumps to three and a half feet would be courting disaster.

How fast you raise criteria is *not* a function of the subject's actual ability, now or in the future; never mind if the horse is a big leggy creature potentially capable of jumping eight feet, or if it habitually hops over four-foot pasture fences. How fast you can raise criteria is a function of how well you are communicating through your shaping procedure what your rules are for gaining reinforcement.

Every time you raise criteria, you are changing the rules. The subject has to be given the opportunity to discover that though the rules have changed, reinforcement can easily continue to be earned by an increase in exertion (and also, in some cases, that performing at the old level no longer works). This can be learned only by experiencing reinforcement at the new level.

If you raise the criteria so high that the subject has to exert itself far beyond anything it has previously done *for you*—regardless of what it does or doesn't do on its own time—you are taking a big risk. The behavior may break down. A jumper might learn bad habits, such as balking or knocking down jumps, habits that will be very time-consuming to eliminate. The fastest way to shape behavior— sometimes the only way—is to raise criteria at whatever interval it takes to make it *easy* for the subject to improve steadily. Constant progress, even if inch by inch, will get you to your ultimate goal much faster than trying to force rapid progress at the risk of losing good performance altogether.

I once saw a father make a serious error in this regard. Because his teenaged son was doing very badly in school, he confiscated the youth's beloved motorcycle until his grades improved. The boy did work harder, and his grades did improve, from Fs and Ds to Ds and Cs. Instead of reinforcing this progress, however, the father said that the grades had not improved *enough* and continued to withhold bike privileges. This escalation of the criteria was too big a jump; the boy stopped working altogether. He furthermore became very mistrustful.

2. *Train one thing at a time; don't try to shape for two criteria simultaneously.*

I don't mean that you can't be working on many different behaviors over the same period of time. Of course you can. In any sort of lesson we might work on form for a while and then on speed—in tennis on the backhand, then the forehand, then footwork, and so on. It relieves monotony. Good teachers vary the work all the time, leaving one task as soon as some progress has been made and going on to another.

While you are working on a given behavior, however, you should work on one criterion at a time, and only that one. If I were training a dolphin to splash and I were to withhold reinforcement one time because the splash was not big enough and the next time because it was in the wrong direction, the animal would have no way of deciphering what I wanted from it. One reinforcement cannot convey two pieces of information: I should shape for size of splash until satisfied with that and then shape for direction of splash, whatever the size, until that, too, is learned; only when both criteria are established could I require both to be obeyed.

This rule has a lot of practical applications. If the task can be broken down into separate components, which are then shaped separately, the learning will go much faster.

Take learning to putt. Putting a golf ball depends on sending it the right distance—not short of the cup and not past it or over it—and sending it in the right direction, not to one side of the cup or the other. If I were going to teach myself to putt, I would practice these separately. Perhaps I would put a piece of tape on the grass, several feet long, and practice hitting the ball just across the tape first from two feet, then four, six, and ten feet, and so on. I might also make a circle of tape, and practice aiming at it from a fixed distance, gradually reducing the circle's size, until I could hit a very small target reliably. Only when I was satisfied with my skills for both distance and direction would I combine them, setting up a large target size and varying the distance, then reducing the target size and varying the distance again until I could hit a small target at many distances. I would then add more criteria, one at a time, such as putting uphill.

This might make me an excellent or even a superb putter, depending on my dedication and the upper limits of my hand-eye coordination. It would certainly, within my capacity, make me a reliable putter. What I am suggesting is that any golfer could improve more in a few weekends following such a single-task shaping program than in a whole summer of random putting practice, hoping willy-nilly to get both the correct distance and the right direction on every shot.

Often when we seem to show no progress in a skill, no matter how much we practice, it is because we are

trying to improve two or more things at once. One needs
to think: Does this behavior have more than one attribute?
Is there some way to break it down and work on different
criteria separately? When you address both of these questions, many problems solve themselves.

3. *Always put the current level of response onto a variable schedule of reinforcement before adding or raising
criteria.*

Remember the variable schedule of reinforcement?
Once a behavior is learned, you must start reinforcing it
only occasionally rather than constantly to maintain it at
the present level. This law is the crux of the shaping
process. When you can afford to reinforce a given level of
behavior only occasionally and still be sure of getting it,
you will be free to use your reinforcements only on the
best examples of the behavior. This selective reinforcement
will "drive" the norm, or average behavior, in the direction
of the improvement you're looking for. Good shaping is a
smooth series of segues between continuous reinforcement—
as a new level is being achieved—and variable reinforcement—as that achievement solidifies and the occasional
even better responses can be reinforced selectively.

Sometimes the alternation between fixed and variable
schedules goes very fast, with just two or three reinforcements at each level. This is particularly apt to happen if
the subject suddenly "gets the picture"—begins understanding what the ultimate goal is and starts improving
spontaneously. Still, the establishment of a variable schedule is so fundamental to shaping that it should never be far
from your awareness and should always be considered if a
shaping program flounders or fails to progress.

4. *When introducing a new criterion, temporarily relax
the old ones.*

Suppose you're learning to play squash, and you've
been working successfully on aim—sending the ball where

you want it to go. Now you'd like to work on speed, but when you hit hard the ball goes every which way. Forget about aim for a while and just slam the ball. When you have achieved some control over the speed of the ball, your aim will come back very quickly.

What is once learned is not forgotten, but under the pressure of assimilating new criteria, old well-learned behavior sometimes falls apart temporarily. I once saw a conductor, during the first dress rehearsal of an opera, having a tantrum because the singers in the chorus were making one musical mistake after another; they seemed virtually to have forgotten all their hard-learned vocal accomplishment. But they were, for the first time, wearing heavy costumes, standing on ladders, being required to move about as they sang: Getting used to new criteria temporarily interfered with previously learned behavior. By the end of the rehearsal, the musical learning reappeared, without coaching. Porpoise trainers call this the "new tank syndrome." When you move a dolphin to a new tank, you have to expect that it will "forget" all it knows until the new stimuli are assimilated. It is important to realize that berating yourself or others for mistakes in past-learned behavior under new circumstances is bad training. The mistakes will usually clear up by themselves shortly, but reprimands cause upset and sometimes tend to draw attention to the mistakes so they *don't* go away.

5. *Stay ahead of your subject.*

Plan your shaping program so that if your subject makes a sudden leap forward you will know what to reinforce next. I once spent two days shaping a newly captured dolphin to jump over a bar a few inches above the water surface. When the behavior was well established, I raised the bar another few inches; the animal jumped immediately and so easily I shortly raised the bar again and by a bigger increment; in fifteen minutes this novice animal was jumping eight feet.

A shaping "breakthrough" of this sort can happen at any time. We see the phenomenon in people, of course, and in many species of intelligent animals. I believe it's due to insight: The subject suddenly realizes the point of what it's being asked to do (in this case, to jump much higher) and goes out and does it. Killer whales are famous for anticipating shaping. Their trainers all have the same joke: You don't have to train killer whales, you just write the behavior on a blackboard and hang it in the water and the whales will follow the script.

Where trainers can run into trouble is if they are not ready for sudden improvement. If you as trainer are going from A to B, and the subject suddenly does B perfectly in two reinforcements, you'd better have in mind steps C and D or you will have nothing further to reinforce.

Breakthroughs often seem to be extremely exciting for the subject; even animals appear to enjoy a kind of "Aha!" experience and often rush about evincing elation. A breakthrough is thus a golden opportunity to make a lot of progress in a hurry. To be unprepared and to hold the subject at a low level of performance just because you don't know what to do next is at best a waste of time and at worst may discourage or disgust your subject so that it becomes less willing to work in the future.

Except under the very best of circumstances, our whole school system seems to be set up to prevent children from learning at their own rate—to penalize not only the slow learners, who don't get the time to learn, but the fast learners, who don't get additional reinforcement when quick thinking moves them ahead. If you understand in a flash what your math teacher is talking about, your reward may be to writhe in boredom for hours, even weeks, while everyone else learns by inches. No wonder street life looks like more fun for the quick ones as well as the slow.

5. *Don't change trainers in midstream.*

While in the midst of shaping a behavior, you risk major slowdowns if you turn the training over to someone else. No matter how scrupulous one may be in discussing criteria before turning over the job, everyone's standards, reaction times, and expectations of progress are slightly different, and the net effect for the subject is to lose reinforcement until those differences can be accommodated.

Of course one trainee may have many different teachers—we have no trouble when one trainer teaches us French, another arithmetic, another football. It is the individual behavior being learned that needs one teacher at a time. During the shaping, or half-learned, stages, consistency of the gradually escalating criteria is best maintained by keeping the shaping of a given behavior in one person's hands. So if, say, you have two children and one dog, and both kids want to teach the dog tricks, let them; but let them each work on separate tricks and spare the poor dog a lot of confusion.

Those who want to learn will learn under the worst of circumstances. One of the by now well-known "ape language" experiments, in which apes are taught vocabularies in American Sign Language and other codes, took place at Columbia University and involved a baby chimpanzee named Nim Chimpsky. Because of budgetary and other problems, the poor creature had more than one hundred "teachers" of signing in a three-year period. The students and experimenters were disappointed that Nim showed no firm evidence of real "language." That is, he apparently never made sentences. But he did learn to recognize and understand more than three hundred signs—nouns, verbs, and so on—which, under the circumstances, I think is amazing. And so some children go from school to school and through the hands of endless processions of substitute teachers and still learn. But there are better ways.

The one time that you should consider changing trainers in midshaping is, of course, when the training is going nowhere. If little or no learning is occurring, you have nothing to lose by switching.

7. *If one shaping procedure is not eliciting progress, try another.*

It is amazing how people will stick to a system that isn't working, convinced somehow that more of the same will get results. No matter what the behavior, there are as many ways to shape it as there are trainers to think them up. In teaching children to swim, for example, one wants to get them to be fearless and comfortable about going underwater. As a first step in this shaping task, one teacher may get them blowing bubbles in the water; another may have them put their faces in quickly and out again; a third may get them bobbing up and down until they dare to bob underneath. Any good teacher, seeing that a child is bored by or afraid of one method, will switch to another; the same shaping methods don't work equally well on every individual.

Traditional trainers, such as circus trainers, often fail to grasp this point. Their shaping procedures have been honed over generations and passed down through families—this is the way you train a bear to ride a bicycle, this is the way you train a lion to roar (tweak a few hairs out of its mane, if you want to know). These traditional "recipes" are considered the best ways, and sometimes they are, but they are also often considered the only ways, which is one reason why circus acts tend to look so much alike.

A TV personality who had done a show at Sea Life Park once in return invited me to visit him and his wife at their farm in Virginia to watch the horse training. This celebrity was an excellent rider and trainer himself and owned a number of performing horses. We were watching a horse being trained to bow, or kneel on one knee, by a traditional method involving two men and a lot of ropes and whips; the horse under this method is repeatedly forced onto one knee until it learns to go down voluntarily.

I said it didn't have to be done that way and asserted that I could train a horse to bow without ever touching the animal (one possibility: Put a red spot on the wall; use food and a conditioned reinforcer to shape the horse to touch its knee to the spot; then lower the spot gradually to the floor so that to touch it correctly and earn reinforcement the horse has to kneel). The TV star became so angry at this impertinent suggestion—the idea! If there were another way to train a bow, he would know about it—that we had to walk him around the outside of the barn two or three times to cool him off.

8. *Don't interrupt a training session gratuitously; that constitutes a punishment.*

This doesn't apply to the casual (though meaningful and productive) shaping one might do around the house—praising schoolwork, welcoming homecomers, encouraging children; a reinforcement here and there, with no formality. In a more formal situation, however—in giving a lesson, say, or in shaping behavior in an animal—the trainer should keep his or her attention on the training subject or the class until the training period is over. This is more than just good manners or good self-discipline; it is good training. When a subject essays to earn reinforcement, it enters into a contract, so to speak, with the trainer. If the trainer starts chatting to some bystander or leaves to answer the telephone or is merely daydreaming, the contract is broken; reinforcement is unavailable through no fault of the trainee. This does more harm than just putting the trainer at risk of missing some good chance for reinforcement. It may have a bad effect on some perfectly good behavior that was going on at the time.

Of course if you *want* to rebuke a subject, removing your attention is a good way to do it. Dolphin trainers call this a "time out" and use it to correct misbehavior. Picking up the fish bucket and walking away for one minute is one of the few ways one has of saying "No!" or "Wrong!" to a dolphin, and it is usually very effective; one wouldn't think dolphins could look chagrined or act contrite, but they can. Removal of attention is a powerful tool, so don't use it carelessly or unfairly.

9. *If a learned behavior deteriorates, review the shaping.*

Sometimes a skill or behavior gets rusty or seems to be totally lost. We all know how it feels to try to speak a language or remember a poem or ride a bicycle if we haven't done it in years and years: It feels most unsettling. Sometimes outside circumstances will temporarily eradicate a well-learned behavior—when stage fright, for instance, makes it impossible to give the thoroughly memorized speech, or a bad fall severely affects your rock-climbing skills. Sometimes subsequent learning overlies or contradicts the original learning, so that mix-ups occur—you strive for the Spanish word and come up with the German.

The quickest way to correct a subject for this kind of deterioration is not to butt at it head on, insisting that the subject get the whole thing back before you're satisfied or before you reinforce, but to recall the original shaping procedure and go all the way through it very rapidly, reinforcing under the new circumstances (twenty years later, in public, whatever) and just reinforcing once or twice at each level. At Sea Life Park we called this "going back to kindergarten," and the technique often brought a poor behavior up to par in ten or fifteen minutes. Of course we are doing just this whenever we review for an exam or refresh our memories by glancing at a script before going onstage. It is useful to remember that if you can more or less match the original shaping process, reviewing works equally well for physical as for mental skills. And it works with animals as well as people.

10. *Quit while you're ahead.*

How long should a shaping session run? That depends partly on the attention span of the subject. Cats often seem to get restless after perhaps a dozen reinforcements, so five minutes might be plenty. Dogs and horses can work longer. Human lessons of many sorts are traditionally an hour long, and football practice, graduate seminars, and various other endeavors often go on all day.

When you stop is not nearly as important as what you stop on. You should *always* quit while you're ahead. This is true for whole sessions, but it also applies to stages within a session, when you stop working on one behavior and go on to another. You should move on on a high note—that is, as soon as some progress has been achieved.

The last behavior that was accomplished is the one that sticks in the subject's mind; you want to be sure it was a good, reinforceable performance. What happens all too often is that we get three or four good responses—the dog retrieves beautifully, the diver does a one-and-a-half for the first time, the singer gets a difficult passage right—and we are so excited that we want to see it again or to do it again. So we repeat it, or try to, and pretty soon the subject is tired, the behavior gets worse, mistakes crop up, corrections and yelling take place, and we just blew a training session. Amateur riders are always doing this. That's why I detest watching people practice jumping their horses; so often they go past the point when they should have stopped, when the animal was doing well and before the behavior began falling apart.

As a trainer you should force yourself, if necessary, to stop on a good response. It takes guts sometimes. But you may find that in the next session the retrieve, the somersault dive, the solo obbligato is not only as good as the last one of the previous session but noticeably better. Psychologists call this "latent learning." Whenever training is going on, some stress is involved, if only the stress of trying to do well. This stress may affect performance enough to mask some of the learning really taking place. At the start of the next session, before stress builds up, the performance may actually begin a step beyond where it left off, and then you have just that much more to reinforce.

Shaping behavior in this way is, of course, the opposite of training by drill and repetition. It can produce not only steady progress but absolutely error-free training, and this can go extremely fast; I once halter-broke a pony yearling in fifteen minutes, from start to finish, and permanently, by moving back and forth between five shaping tasks (forward, stop, left, right, and back) while reinforcing progress in each one. Accomplishing such speedy training depends, paradoxically, on your willingness to give up time limits, specific goal setting, and speed of progress itself as a goal. You must instead count simply on your willingness to quit while you're ahead. A Zen phenomenon.

Sometimes you can't end each training session on a high note. Perhaps the students paid for an hour and they want an hour, though a good quitting time was reached earlier. Or perhaps the session really isn't going well enough to provide a high point, but fatigue is soon going to be a problem. In that case it is wise to end the session with some easy, guaranteed way to earn reinforcement so that the session as a whole is remembered as being reinforcing. Dolphin trainers often end long, demanding sessions with a bit of easy ball playing; riding teachers sometimes use games such as "Simon Says" or tag. The most inadvisable technique is to introduce new tasks or material late in the session so that it concludes with a series of inadequate and unreinforced behaviors. My piano lessons, as a child, always ended this way; it was very discouraging and I still can't play the piano.

The Training Game

Even if you know and understand the principles of shaping, you can't apply them unless you practice them. Shaping is not a verbal process, it is a nonverbal skill—a flow of interactive behavior through time, like dancing, or making love, or surfing. As such, it can't really be learned by reading or thinking or talking about it. You have to do it.

One easy and fascinating way to develop shaping skills is by playing the Training Game. I use the Training Game in teaching the techniques of training. Many trainers play it for sport; it makes an interesting party game.

You need two people at least: the subject and the trainer. Six is ideal because then every person can experience being both subject and trainer at least once before the group gets tired; but larger groups—a classroom or lecture audience, for example—are feasible, because observing is almost as much fun as participating.

You send the subject out of the room. The rest of the people select a trainer and choose a behavior to be shaped: for example, to write one's name on the blackboard, jump up and down, or stand on a chair. The subject is invited back in and told to move about the room and be active; the trainer reinforces, by blowing on a whistle, movements in the general direction of the desired behavior. I like to make a rule at least for the first few reinforcements that the "animal" has to go back to the doorway after each reinforcement and start anew; it seems to help prevent a tendency of some subjects to just stand still wherever reinforcement was last received. And no talking. Laughter, groans, and other signs of emotion are permitted, but instructions and discussion are out until after the behavior is achieved.

Ordinarily the Training Game goes quite fast. Here's an example: Six of us are playing the game in a friend's living room. Ruth volunteers to be the animal, and it's Anne's turn to be the trainer. Ruth goes out of the room. We all decide that the behavior should be to turn on the lamp on the end table beside the couch.

Ruth is called back in and begins wandering around the room. When she heads in the direction of the lamp, Anne blows the whistle. Ruth goes back to "Start" (the doorway), then moves purposefully to the spot where she was reinforced and stops. No whistle. She waves her hands about. No whistle. She moves off the spot, tentatively, away from the lamp as it happens. Still hearing no whistle,

Ruth begins walking around again. When once again she walks toward the lamp, Anne blows the whistle.

Ruth returns to the door and then returns to the new spot where she just heard the whistle, but this time she keeps walking forward. Bingo: whistle. Without going back to the door, she walks forward some more and hears the whistle just as she is coming up against the end table. She stops. She bumps the end table. No whistle. She waves her hands around; no whistle. One hand brushes the lampshade, and Anne whistles. Ruth begins touching the lampshade all over—moving it, turning it, rocking it: no whistle. Ruth reaches up underneath the lampshade. Whistle. Ruth reaches underneath the shade again, and, the gesture being very familiar and having a purpose, she executes the purpose and turns on the lamp. Anne whistles and the rest of us applaud.

Things don't always go that smoothly, even with simple, familiar behaviors. Anne, as it turned out, made a good training decision when she withheld reinforcement as Ruth moved from the spot where she'd first been reinforced, but in the wrong direction. If, however, Ruth had then moved back to the spot and just stood there, Anne might have been in trouble.

Here's an example of a round of the Training Game that presented more of a problem. I was teaching training in a high school class. Leonard was the animal and Beth the trainer. The behavior was to turn on the ceiling lights, this time with a wall switch.

Leonard came into the room and began moving about, and Beth quickly shaped him to go to the wall where the light switch was. However, Leonard had started out with his hands in his pockets; after several reinforcements for moving about with his hands in his pockets, they were stuck there as if glued. He bumped the wall, he turned and leaned on the wall, he even leaned on the light switch, but the switch seemed to be invisible to him and he never took his hands out of his pockets.

As I watched, I thought that if Leonard could be

nduced to feel the wall with a hand, he would notice the switch and turn on the light. But how to get those hands out of the pockets? Beth had another idea. She "caught" with the whistle a bent-knees movement while Leonard had his back to the wall and soon had shaped him to rub his back up and down on the wall near the switch. The other students giggled as they realized that by shifting the movement sideways Beth might get Leonard to move the switch with his back, thus meeting the criterion accidentally, if not deliberately. But it was a slow business, and we could see that Leonard was getting frustrated and angry.

"Can I try?" asked Maria. Beth glanced at me for approval, I shrugged, the class seemed to acquiesce, and Maria got out her own whistle (acquiring a whistle was the only course requirement). Maria waved Leonard back to the "Start" position at the door and then moved a chair near the light switch, about a foot out from the wall, sat down on it herself, and nodded to Leonard to begin. He headed briskly for the wall where he had been reinforced so often, passing Maria and apparently ignoring her new position. As he passed her, she stuck out her foot and tripped him.

Leonard's hands flew out of his pockets and against the wall, to break his fall; as the hands hit, the whistle blew. Leonard froze. He looked at Maria. She gazed into the middle distance, to avoid cuing him in any way. Tentatively he began patting the wall; she reinforced that. He patted the wall again, and this time he looked at what he was doing; she reinforced that. Then we all saw Leonard focus abruptly on the light switch. No one breathed. He straightened his spine a little, suddenly full of awareness, and switched on the lights. Tumultuous applause.

Everyone involved in the Training Game, participants and spectators alike, learns from almost every reinforcement. The trainer, first of all, gets to discover what timing is all about. Suppose the subject approaches the light switch, but just as the trainer blows the whistle, the

subject turns away. Well, thinks the trainer, I'll catch
next time. But now suppose the subject goes back to th
starting point, then hurries toward the switch and whir
away from it. Groan. The trainer has shaped that whir
And everyone, not just the trainer, sees how crucial it is t
get the whistle in a little earlier, while the desired behav
ior is actually occurring.

The subject gets to discover that in this form of learn
ing, brains don't help. It doesn't matter what you ar
thinking about; if you just keep moving around, collectin
whistle sounds, your body will find out what to do withou
"your" help. This is an absolutely excruciating experienc
for brilliant, intellectual people. They tend to freeze whe
they hear the whistle and to try to analyze what they wer
doing. That they don't know, and that it doesn't matte
that they don't know, is a shocker. A colleague, She
Gish, and I once trained psychologist Ronald Schusterma
to walk around the room with his hands clenched behin
his back for periods of up to a minute—a long time to g
without a reinforcement, but he was diligent—until th
assembled room agreed that we had the behavior thor
oughly established, and burst into applause (that is th
reinforcement for the trainer, incidentally, and it almos
always occurs spontaneously). Ron, who trains many an
mals in his research, and who had rashly opined that h
himself "could not be trained," was unaware that hi
clenched fists behind his back were now a shaped behav
ior, not just a subliminal expression of opinion.

What this demonstrates is not some Machiavellia
nature of reinforcement training but the hazards in ou
habitual error of assuming that verbal communication i
all-important, and that learning cannot take place withou
the use of language or at least some verbal consciousness
The experience of nonverbal learning is especially usefu
for people who do a lot of verbal instructing in thei
professional lives: teachers, therapists, supervisors. Onc
you have been the "animal" you can sympathize, eve
empathize, with any subject that is exhibiting the behavio

you are shaping but has not yet *comprehended* what it is supposed to be doing, so that it easily makes mistakes. You can have patience with the animal (or the child or patient) that explodes in frustration and rage when what it had confidently thought was the right thing to do turns out to be no good, a contretemps that can bring human subjects close to tears. And once you have performed nonverbal shaping with adult human subjects in an exercise, you may not be so quick to say in a teaching, coaching, or training situation in real life that the subject (animal, student, whatever) "hates me," or "is deliberately trying to get my goat," or "is stupid," or "must be sick today." It is patently obvious, during this exercise in which everyone is participating by agreement and with a will, that whatever goes wrong is a function of the training, not the trainee.

The illumination this game provides for professionals is part of the fun (and everyone else gets your insights at the same time—you can't hide, but on the other hand you are bathed in amused sympathy). A charm of the game purely as entertainment is that anyone can play it without previous experience. Some people have a wonderful knack for it. In my experience, intuitive, creative, intensely emotional people make great shapers, and calm, observant people make great animals—just the opposite of what you might expect. Finally, one has only to look at a roomful of people intent on the shaping going on, with everyone motionless but the subject, and the trainer's whole body and mind focused on the task, to see that this is an experience akin to painting or writing: It is creative work. Except on stage, creativity is rarely shared as a group experience. The Training Game is valuable for that aspect alone.

We played some memorable rounds of the Training Game at Sea Life Park, especially one in which philosopher Gregory Bateson, being the "animal" for some of my porpoise trainers, proved indeed to be impossible to train, not because he stood still and thought but because he offered such an endless variety of responses that the trainer was swamped. Another to me very interesting round of this game occurred following a luncheon of six professional women, mostly unknown to each other and from widely unrelated fields. After two hours of the game, in which a psychotherapist proved to be a marvelous "animal" and a disco dancer a brilliant shaper, we left knowing each other much better and liking each other a good deal, too.

In 1980 I taught an experimental course in training to a group of high school students at the Brearley School in New York City. We played the Training Game in class, and a hard core of half a dozen fiendishly imaginative young women began playing the Training Game at home among themselves, working in pairs usually, and shaping exotic behaviors such as crawling upstairs backward. They had been taught—successfully, in my opinion—to think analytically at the Brearley School, and they correctly did their hard thinking before and after a shaping session and flung themselves into the shaping itself with the normal gusto of sixteen-year-olds. In no time they were shaping parents, using positive reinforcement on teachers, and turning obnoxious siblings into amusing companions by selectively reinforcing desired behavior. I never saw a group, before or since, grasp both the techniques and their possibilities so rapidly.

Shaping Shortcuts: Targeting, Mimicry, and Modeling

Professional trainers use a number of techniques to make shaping go faster. Three that may be of use to you are targeting, mimicry, and modeling.

In targeting, which is widely used in the training of sea lions and other performing animals, you shape the animal to touch its nose to a target—a knob on the end of a pole, say, or often simply the trainer's closed fist. Then, by moving the target around and getting the animal merely to go and touch it, you can elicit all kinds of other behavior, such as climbing stairs, jumping or rearing up, following the trainer, getting into and out of a shipping crate, and so on. We are essentially using targeting when we slap our thighs to coax a dog to us. The movement seems to attract dogs, and when they approach we reinforce the behavior with petting. Patting the couch to invite someone to sit beside you is a form of targeting. Japanese tourist groups stick together among crowds of much taller people by following a flag held above the crowd by their tour leaders—again, targeting. Flags and banners have traditionally served the same purpose in battle.

Mimicry comes naturally to some animals and birds, as well as to people. Young creatures of all sorts learn much of what they need to know by watching and then copying the behavior of their elders. While "learning by observation" is often taken by psychologists as a sign of intelligence in animals—primates being good at it and some other animals poor—I think the presence or absence of this skill in a species is a function of its ecology—that is, of its role in nature—rather than of intelligence per se. Some birds are remarkably good at behavioral mimicry. Titmice in England learned to open milk bottles on doorsteps and drink the cream, a skill which, through mimicry, spread so rapidly through the titmouse population that milk-bottle tops had to be redesigned.

Dogs are *not* good at learning by observation; when they do what other dogs are doing, it is usually because they are responding to the same stimuli, not because they are mimicking. On the other hand, cats, which get lower "IQ scores" than dogs from the animal psychologists, are wonderful mimickers. The folk expression "copycat" is no accident. If you teach a trick—ringing the doorbell to be let in, say—to one cat in the household, new or other cats may well learn it with no training from you. Cats will even copy noncats. One evening my daughter spent an hour teaching her poodle to sit on a child's rocking chair and rock it, using chopped ham as the reinforcement. One of the cats was watching. When the lesson was over the cat, unprompted, got on the chair and rocked it most correctly, looking up for its own share of chopped ham, which it most certainly had earned.

I think this strong tendency to mimic explains why cats get stuck in trees. Climbing up comes more or less automatically: It is, as biologists say, "hard-wired." The claws stick out and the cat runs up the tree. To get down, however, the cat has to descend backward, so that its down-curved claws can still operate, and this appears to be a learned, or "soft-wired," skill. I can testify to this because I have personally (in the middle of the night, and on top of a ladder) shaped a cat to come down a tree backward. I did so in order to spare myself the mournful yowls of a stuck cat in the future, and indeed the cat stayed shaped—it never got stuck again (though it continued to climb trees). I think in nature cats learn how to turn around and descend backward from watching their mothers as they climb trees together, but because we take them from their mothers at such a tender age—six to eight weeks—this opportunity for copycatting is lost.

Dolphins have a strong tendency to mimic one another, which facilitates training. To get several dolphins doing the same thing you shape the behavior in one, then reinforce the others for any attempt to copy. In captivity baby dolphins often learn the adults' tricks long before they themselves are old enough for fish rewards, and many oceanariums have had the experience of "understudies," animals on the sidelines that watch other performing animals and prove to have learned the show behaviors without ever being reinforced for them or even doing them. For wild dolphins, apparently, being able to imitate other dolphins must be important for survival.

We can and should use mimicry wherever possible in teaching physical skills to humans—dancing, skiing, tennis, and so on. It's usually wise for the person giving the sample behavior to stand beside or turn his or her back to the subjects, so they can follow the motions with their own bodies without having to do any mental translating. The less deciphering needed, and the less verbal description used, the better the mimicry will work. Incidentally, if you want to teach a right-handed skill (crocheting, say) to a left-handed person, you should sit facing him or her and have the subject mimic you, thus executing not the same-sided movements but a mirror image.

Of course a major part of the shaping of the behavior of our children takes place through mimicry. What they see us do, they do too, for better or worse. In my post office one morning recently, three little children were making such a ruckus it was hard to hear anything else. Their mother, waiting in line, yelled at them several times before she succeeded in frightening them into silence. "How *do* you get kids to be quiet?" she asked the postmistress. "Try speaking softly yourself," the postmistress said, quite correctly. Columnist Judith Martin ("Miss Manners") suggests, when teaching good manners to children, that during the training period—"from birth to marriage" —everybody else in the house will have to eat tidily, speak civilly, and at least feign interest in the doings and conversation of others.

The third shaping shortcut, modeling, consists of pushing the subject manually through the action we want that subject to learn. A golfer does this when he puts his arms around the novice from behind, holds the club, and moves the club and the subject in the desired swing. Some of those who teach sign language to apes employ a lot of modeling. The trainer holds the young chimpanzee's hands and puts them in the desired positions or movements; eventually the ape is supposed to get the picture and make the movements spontaneously. Modeling was the secret of "living statues," a circus act very popular around the turn of the century in which live people and horses were posed to resemble famous paintings or sculptures. The effect that audiences loved was the motionlessness. When the lights went up, there they all were, Napoleon's troops at Waterloo or whatever, caught as if in mid-movement—not just the men, but the horses, too, with necks arched, forelegs in midair, as if turned to stone. It was done, I am told, by massaging the horses for hours until they were utterly relaxed, and then modeling them like clay into the desired poses, and reinforcing them for staying there.

I am always a little dubious about modeling as a training device, even though it is widely used. Until the subject is doing the behavior or at least trying to do the behavior without being held or pushed or modeled, I am not sure much learning takes place. Often all the subject learns is to let you put it through the motions: The dog, being taught to retrieve, learns to let you hold its mouth shut with the dumbbell in its jaws, but when you let go, it lets go; the toddler, put firmly into a high chair, sits quietly while you hold him or her but is up and moving the minute you take your hand away. It's the modeler who gets trained—to hold or guide for longer and longer periods.

It would seem that by putting a subject through the same motions long enough, or often enough, eventually it would learn how to do the behavior. Sometimes this is true, but eventually can be a long time away, and to go from being pushed through a movement to doing it yourself requires insight: "Aha! They want *ME* to do this myself." This is an awful lot to ask of an animal. And even if your subject is an Einstein, repetition in the hope that enlightenment will strike is an inefficient use of valuable training time. The way to make modeling work is to combine it with shaping. While you are putting the subject in position, or through the motions, you stay sensitive to the smallest effort on the subject's part to initiate the proper motion, and that effort is the behavior you reinforce. The dog's jaws tighten on the dumbbell ever so slightly, the golfer begins to swing smoothly, the little chimp's hands move of themselves, and you praise that moment. Then you can shape the new skill while "fading" away the modeling. The combination of modeling and shaping is often an effective way of training behavior; but it is the combination that works and not the modeling alone.

Special Subjects

You can shape behavior in just about any organism. Psychologists have shaped tiny babies to wave their arms to make the lights in the room go off and on. You can shape birds. You can shape fish. I shaped a large hermit crab once to ring a dinner bell by pulling on a string with its claw. (The trick was to get the food to the crab the instant its claw, waving about aimlessly, connected with the string; I used a long pair of dissecting forceps to put bits of shrimp right into the crab's mouthparts.) Harvard professor Richard Herrnstein told me he once shaped a scallop to clap its shell for a food reward. (He didn't tell me how he got the food to the scallop.) Marine-mammal trainers like to boast that they can shape *any* animal to do *anything* it is physically and mentally capable of doing, and as far as I can tell, they can.

One of the effects of shaping sessions, especially if they are fruitful experiences for the subject, is to increase attention span; actually you are shaping duration of participation. However, some organisms naturally do not have long attention spans. Immature organisms—puppies, foals, babies—should never be asked for more than three or four repetitions of a given behavior; pressure beyond that may discourage or frighten. This is not to say that immature organisms can't learn. They are learning all the time, but in brief snatches. A fishing captain I know taught his four-month-old granddaughter to "Gimme five!" and the baby's enthusiastic open-handed slap of his palm, in a tiny simulacrum of the jazz musician's greeting, was a never-failing hit with spectators. But he did it in only a few almost momentary "training sessions."

Infancy is not the only biological constraint affecting shaping. Some behaviors come naturally to some species and are difficult for others. Pigs, for example, seem to find it hard to carry something about in their jaws but easy to learn to shove things with their snouts. Most breeds of dogs have been developed for behavioral tendencies as well as looks: One hardly needs to shape a collie to herd sheep, since the necessary stalking behavior has been established, even exaggerated, by breeding; but you'd be giving yourself a tough assignment if you decided to shape sheepherding in a basset hound. Some skills are more easily learned at particular stages of development; a baby mongoose may be tamed and turned into a delightful pet up to the age of six weeks but not after that. Humans are generally thought to acquire languages more easily as children than as adults, although linguists have recently found that an adult who is willing to work at it can probably learn a new language faster than most children and teenagers. One behavior I think is really very difficult to teach to humans in adulthood is swimming. We are among the very few species that do not swim naturally, and while you can teach an adult to float, and to make the proper strokes, I have never seen anyone who can frolic and be at ease in deep water unless he or she learned to swim in childhood.

How about shaping yourself? All kinds of programs exist for changing one's own behavior: SmokEnders, Weight Watchers, and so on. Most such programs draw heavily on shaping methods, usually called behavior modification, and they may or may not be successful. The difficulty, I think, is that they require you to reinforce yourself. But when you are reinforcing yourself, the event is never a surprise—the subject always knows what the trainer is up to. This makes it awfully easy to say "The heck with getting another star on my chart, I'd rather have a cigarette."

The evidence suggests that any program for self-shaping may work for some people. Other people may be successful only after going through three or four different programs, or several repetitions of a given method. Such people can in fact successfully change a habit or give up an addiction, but hardly ever on the first try. Still others may be helped enormously by some form of hypnosis or self-hypnosis. A senior editor at a big publishing house told me that he was able to kick a major cigarette habit by learning, from a hypnotist, to relax into a light trance through self-hypnosis, and to repeat as a mantra or charm a phrase such as "I do not want to smoke" whenever he felt an overpowering urge. For him, as he put it, this technique seemed to "drop a curtain" between him and the cigarette; relief and self-congratulation when the urge had passed was the reinforcement. Perhaps such hypnotic techniques enlist the subconscious mind as the trainer, allowing some separation from the subject, which is the conscious mind, and thus making both negative and positive reinforcement more effective.

Out of curiosity, while writing this book, I tried out some formal shaping programs, two classroom-taught and two self-administered, for quitting smoking and for learning meditation, weight control, and money management. All were moderately successful but not necessarily at first; some took well over a year. The single most useful device in self-reinforcement, I found, was record keeping, which all four programs made use of. I needed to record performance in such a way that *improvement* could be seen at a glance. I used graphs. Thus my guilt over a lapse could be assuaged by looking at the graphs and seeing that, even so, I was doing much better now than I had been six months previously. Perfection might still be a long way off, but the "curve," or sloping line, of the graph was in the right direction, and this visible proof of improvement, while itself a weak and slow-operating reinforcement, did provide enough motivation to keep me going most of the time.

One kind of self-administered shaping that works beautifully is training by computer. Amusing reinforcements can be built into the computer program so that learning proceeds fast and the shaping experience is fun. It has become an extremely promising application of the laws of positive reinforcement.

Shaping Without Words

In formal training situations, such as a tennis lesson, the subject knows he or she is being shaped and is usually a willing party to the procedure. Thus you don't have to just wait for the response and reinforce it. You can use words to prompt the behavior, and without harm: "Do this. Good. Now do it twice. Good."

In informal situations in real life, however, you are probably better off shaping without instructions or verbal discussion. Suppose you have a messy roommate who leaves dirty clothes all over the place, and verbal instructions—scolding, pleading, whatever—haven't worked. Can you shape neatness? Possibly.

You would of course draw up a shaping plan, the initial and intermediate steps by which you would reach the desired goal. To get dirty clothes into the hamper every time, for example, you might start with one sock, once, and "target" the behavior by holding out the open hamper just as the sock is about to go on the floor. Reinforcement can be verbal, tactile, or whatever you think the roommate would be likely to respond to or accept. People are not dumb; they modify their behavior on just a handful of reinforcements. Even if the scattering of dirty clothes is actually an act of subtle aggression directed against you ("Pick up my clothes, peon!"), by using positive reinforcement you can shape a steady and visible progress toward whatever you consider an adequate level of tidiness.

There are, however, two traps in this use of shaping. The first is that it is easier to notice mistakes than to notice improvement, so, verbal creatures that we are, it is much easier for us to remonstrate when criteria are not met than to reinforce when they are. And that can undo the progress. The second trap is that if you are calculating to shape someone's behavior, it is very tempting to talk about it. And talking about it can ruin it. If you say, "I am going to reinforce you"—for putting your laundry in the hamper, for not smoking marijuana, for spending less, or whatever—you are bribing or promising, not actually reinforcing; on learning of your plans, the person may rebel, instantly, and escalate misbehavior. To get results, you have to *do* the shaping, not talk about it.

And if you do achieve success in shaping someone else's behavior, you better not brag about it later, either. Some people never catch on to this and will insist on showing off what "they" did—patronizing at best, and a great way to make a lifelong enemy of the subject. Besides, while you may have helped someone improve a skill or get rid of a bad habit by changing your behavior in order to reinforce appropriately, who actually did all the hard work? The subject. Wise parents never go around talking about what a good job they did raising their kids. For one thing, we all know the job is never over, and for another, the kids deserve the credit—if only for surviving all the training mistakes we made.

Because the shaping of people can or even must be tacit, it smacks to some people of an evil sort of manipulativeness. I think this is a misunderstanding. The reason the shaping needs to be nonverbal is that it is behavior we are working with, not ideas, and not just the subjects' behavior but yours as well.

However: Since you can shape people's behavior without their conscious awareness that you are doing so, and since, outside of the formal agreement to be shaped, as in a tennis lesson, you almost have to shape human behavior on the nonverbal level, then isn't it possible to shape people to do horrible things?

Yes, indeed, especially if you are using, as negative reinforcement, an aversive stimulus so severe as to cause real fear, even terror. Psychologists have discovered in the laboratory a phenomenon called "learned helplessness." If an animal is taught to avoid an aversive stimulus, such as an electric shock, by pressing a lever or moving to another part of the cage, and is then placed in a cage where there is absolutely no way it can avoid the shock, it will gradually give up trying. It will become completely malleable and passive, and may even lie there and accept punishment when the way to freedom is once again open. "Brainwashing" is possibly a related phenomenon in people. If a person is subjected to severe deprivation and inescapable fear or pain, and if the aversive stimuli are subsequently used as negative reinforcement—that is, as contingencies that the subject can avoid or cause to desist by a change in behavior—well, then . . . animals tend to go to pieces, but people are tougher, and some will do anything they need to to avoid the negative reinforcement. Let the photographs of Patty Hearst, holding a machine gun in a bank robbery, be evidence. But while her captors did not need a book to tell them how to do that, would we not all be better defended against such events if we understood, each of us, how the laws of shaping work?

3
Stimulus Control: Cooperation Without Coercion

Stimuli

Anything that causes some kind of behavioral response is called a stimulus. Some stimuli can cause responses without any learning or training: We flinch at a loud noise, blink at a bright light, and tend to wander into the kitchen when appetizing smells waft out to us; animals would do the same. Such sounds, lights, and scents are called unconditioned, or primary, stimuli.

Other stimuli are learned by association. They may be meaningless in themselves, but they have become recognizable signals for behavior: Traffic lights make us stop and go, we leap to answer ringing telephones, on a noisy street we turn at the sound of our own names, and so on and on. In any given day we respond to a multitude of learned signals. These are called conditioned, or secondary, stimuli.

An enormous part of most formal training efforts consists of establishing conditioned stimuli. The drill sergeant with a platoon of recruits and the dog owner in a training class are equally and primarily concerned with getting trainees to obey commands, which are actually conditioned stimuli. It's not impressive that a dog can sit or a man can halt; what is impressive is that it is done with precision and on command. That is what we call obedience—not merely the acquisition of behaviors but the guarantee that they will be executed when the signal is given. Psychologists call this "bringing behavior under stimulus control." It is hard to train, the training follows rules, and the rules are worth examination.

What if you don't care to boss some dog around and never in your life plan to train a drill team? You can still make use of an understanding of stimulus control. For example, if your kids dawdle and don't come when you call, you have poor stimulus control. If you supervise people, and you sometimes have to give an order or instruction two or three times before it gets done, you have a stimulus-control problem. Did you ever hear these words come out of your mouth: "If I've told you once, I've told you a thousand times, don't . . ." (slam the door, or leave your wet bathing suit on the couch, or whatever)? When telling once *or* a thousand times isn't working, the behavior is not under stimulus control.

We may think we have stimulus control when actually we don't. We expect a signal or command to be obeyed in such cases and it isn't. One common human reaction is to escalate the signal. The waiter doesn't understand your French? Speak louder. Usually this doesn't work. The subject has to recognize the signal; otherwise it doesn't matter if you yell, or blare it through a rock-band amplification system, you'll still get a blank stare. Another human reaction to failure to get a response to a conditioned stimulus is to get mad. This works only if the subject is deliberately disobeying by not giving a well-learned response to a well-learned cue. Then sometimes a show of temper can elicit good behavior.

Sometimes the subject responds correctly but after a delay or in a dilatory manner. Often a sluggish response to commands is due to the fact that the subject has not been taught to respond quickly. Without positive reinforcement, not only for the correct response to a cue but also for prompt response, the subject has had no chance to learn that there are benefits in quick obedience to signals. The behavior really isn't under stimulus control.

Real life abounds in bad management of stimulus control. Whenever one person is trying to exert authority, another person is likely to be getting into trouble for "disobedience"; but the real problem is commands that are not understood or signals that can't be obeyed—poor communication or sloppy stimulus control.

The Rules of Stimulus Control

To establish stimulus control, you shape a behavior and then in effect shape the offering of this behavior during or right after some particular stimulus. That stimulus then becomes the cue, or signal, for the behavior.

For example, let's suppose you have made your dog sit by pressing down on its rump and pulling up on the collar. These are unconditioned stimuli; they work without having to be learned. You then reinforce any voluntary cooperation, shaping the behavior of sitting. You do this while saying "Sit," which at first means nothing to the dog (any word in any language will do, of course). When the dog has learned that sometimes you want him to sit, he can then absorb the task of sitting during or after the presentation of the signal, or conditioned stimulus, of "Sit." Finally he sits, promptly and with confidence, when he is told to.

Now the behavior is under stimulus control, right? Wrong. Only half the job is done. The animal must also be trained—and it is a separate training task—not to sit when it has not been given the command. Bringing behavior under stimulus control is not accomplished until the behavior is also extinguished in the absence of the conditioned stimulus.

This does not mean, of course, that the dog must stand up all day unless you say "Sit." The subject can do what it pleases on its own time. It is in the training or working situation, where conditioned stimuli, or cues and signals, are going to be used, that both the "go" and the "no-go" aspects of a signal must be established if performance is to be reliable.

Complete, perfect stimulus control is defined by four conditions, each one of which may have to be approached as a separate training task, a separate item in the shaping recipe:

1. The behavior always occurs immediately upon presentation of the conditioned stimulus (the dog sits when told to).
2. The behavior never occurs in the absence of the stimulus (during a training or work session the dog never sits spontaneously).
3. The behavior never occurs in response to some other stimulus (if you say "Lie down," the dog does not offer the sit instead).
4. No other behavior occurs in response to this stimulus (when you say "Sit," the dog does not respond by lying down or by leaping up and licking your face).

Only when all four conditions are met does the dog really, fully, and finally understand the command "Sit!" Now you have real stimulus control.

Where, in real life, do we use or need such complete stimulus control? In music, for one example. Orchestra conductors often make very complex use of stimulus control, and, in turn, a conductor in rehearsal may come upon every possible kind of response error. He may, for example, signal for a response—"forte," more volume, say— and not get it, perhaps because he has not yet clearly established the meaning of the signal. Or he may avoid signaling for more volume and get too much sound anyway. The brass section of classical orchestras is famous for this; Richard Strauss, in a satiric list of rules for young conductors, said, "Never look encouragingly at the brass players." The conductor may signal for another behavior—

"Presto," perhaps—and instead of getting faster music, the conductor gets more volume: Tenor soloists seem to do this a lot. Finally, the conductor may ask for more volume and instead get a lot of mistakes: Amateur choruses do this. Each kind of error in response to the conditioned stimulus must be corrected, by training, before the conductor will be satisfied that he or she has adequate stimulus control.

Stimulus control is also vital in the military. The training of rookies in close-order drill, a laborious and time-consuming business, may seem both difficult and meaningless to the recruits, but it has an important function. Not only does it establish prompt response to marching commands, which enables the leaders to move large groups of men about efficiently, but it also trains the skill of learning to respond to conditioned stimuli in general: obedience to command, which is after all not just a state of mind but a learned ability, constituting a crucial and often lifesaving skill to a soldier. Ever since armies were invented, close-order drill has been a way of training this skill.

What Kind of Signal?

A conditioned stimulus—a learned signal—can be anything, absolutely anything, that the subject is capable of perceiving. Flags, lights, words, touch, vibration, popping champagne corks . . . it simply doesn't matter what kind of signal you use. As long as the subject can sense it, the signal can be used to elicit learned behavior.

Dolphins are usually trained with visual hand signals, but I know of a blind dolphin that learned to offer many behaviors in response to being touched in various ways. Sheep dogs are usually trained with hand signals and voice commands. In New Zealand, however, where the countryside is wide and the dog may be far off, the conditioned stimuli are often piercing whistles, which carry farther than voice commands. When a shepherd in New Zealand sells such a dog, the buyer may live many miles away with no way to write down whistles, the old owner teaches the new owner the commands over the telephone.

Fish will condition to sounds or lights—we all know how fish in an aquarium rush to the top when you tap the glass or turn on the light. And human beings will condition to practically anything.

It is useful, in a working situation, to condition all subjects to the same cues and signals, so that other people can elicit the same behavior. Thus animal trainers tend to be quite traditional about the conditioned stimuli they use. All over the world horses go forward when you kick their ribs and halt when you pull on the reins. The camels at the Bronx Zoo lie down when they're told "Cush!" even though no one around them, including their trainer, speaks Arabic; everybody just knows that's how you're supposed to tell a camel to lie down. That New York camels could just as well learn to lie down on hearing "Cool it, baby" doesn't matter.

Traditional trainers, therefore, often fail to realize that many conditioned stimuli are arbitrary. Once at a boarding stables I was working with a young horse on a lead line, teaching it "Walk!" as a command. The trainer at the stables looked on with disgust and finally said, "You can't do it that way—horses don't understand 'walk'; you have to say 'Tch, tch'!" Taking the rope from my hand he said, "Tch, tch," and popped the colt on the rump with the loose rope end, which naturally made the horse start forward. "See?" he said, point proved.

I saw. From then on, wherever I boarded my ponies, I trained them to respond not only to my commands, but to whatever set of giddyaps, gees, haws, and whoas were used by the trainer in charge. It saved trouble, and it made them think I was quite a promising amateur trainer. At least I didn't have my signals crossed!

It was not only possible but easy to train the ponies to two sets of commands. While you don't want more than one behavior occurring on a single stimulus, it's perfectly feasible to have several conditioned stimuli for one behavior. For example, in a crowded room a speaker can ask for quiet by shouting "Quiet" or by standing up and raising one hand in a gesture meaning "Hush." Or, if the occupants of the room are both noisy and slightly drunk, consequently inattentive, banging a spoon on a water glass will work. We're all conditioned to give this one behavior in response to any of at least three stimuli.

Establishing a second conditioned stimulus for a learned behavior is called transferring the stimulus. To make a transfer you present the old stimulus—a voice command, perhaps—as usual, and the new one—a hand signal, say—while reinforcing the response; then you gradually make the old stimulus less and less obvious while calling attention to the new one by making it very obvious, until the response is given equally well to the new stimulus, even without giving the old one at all. This usually goes quite a bit faster than the training of the original signal; since "Do this behavior" and "Do this behavior on command" have already been established, "Do this behavior on another command, too" is more easily learned.

Signal Magnitude and Fading

Conditioned stimuli do not have to be of any particular volume or size to get results. A primary, or unconditioned, stimulus produces a gradation of results, depending on its intensity; one reacts more vigorously to a sharp jab than to a pinprick, and the louder the noise, the more it startles. A conditioned stimulus, however, merely has to be recognized to elicit the full response. You see a red light and you stop the car; you don't stop faster or slower depending on the size of the light fixture. As long as you recognize the signal you know what to do. Therefore, once a stimulus has been learned, it is possible not only to transfer it but also to make it smaller and smaller, until it is barely perceptible, and still get the same results. Eventually you can get results with a signal so small that it cannot be perceived by a bystander. This is called "fading" the stimulus.

We use fading all the time: What has to be a very broad stimulus at first ("No, Dickie, we do not put sand in other children's hair," as you remove Dickie forcibly from the sandbox) becomes, with time, a small signal (merely a lifted eyebrow or wagged index finger). Animal trainers sometimes get wonderful, apparently magical results with faded stimuli. One of the funniest acts I've seen involved a parrot at the San Diego Wild Animal Park which cackled in hysterical laughter in response to a tiny movement of the trainer's hand. You can see the possibilities: "Pedro, what do you think of this man's hat?" "Hahahahaha. . . ." Because the audience did not see the signal, the parrot's single learned behavior seemed the product of a sardonic intelligence cuttingly answering the question; actually, it was a well-timed response to a well-faded stimulus, and the sardonic intelligence, if any, belonged to the trainer, or maybe the scriptwriter.

By far the best examples of conditioning, fading, and transferring stimuli I have seen occur not in the world of animal training but in symphony rehearsal halls. As an amateur singer I have worked in several opera and symphony choruses, often under guest conductors. While many of the signals conductors give to musicians are more or less standardized, each conductor has personal signals as well, and the meaning of these must be established in a very short time—rehearsal time often barely exceeds performance time. Once, in a rehearsal of Mahler's *"Resurrection" Symphony*, just as the basses were about to make their usual booming entrance, I watched the conductor establish an unconditioned stimulus for "Come in softly" by miming an expression of wild alarm and crouching with a hand thrown across his face as if to ward off a blow. Everyone got the message, and in the next few minutes the conductor was able to fade the stimulus, reducing volume in any section of the chorus with a warning glance and a bit of a crouch, or a fleeting echo of the hand gesture, and finally with just a flinch of the shoulder. Conductors also often transfer stimuli by combining a known or obvious gesture—an upward movement of the palm for "Louder," say—with an unknown gesture such as a personal tilt of the head or turn of the body. Sitting on the conductor's left in the alto section I once saw a guest conductor momentarily transfer all the altos' louder-softer signals to his left elbow.

One result of establishing stimulus control is that the subject must become attentive if it wants to get reinforced for responding correctly, especially if the stimuli are faded. In fact the subject may eventually be able to perceive signals so subtle that the trainer is not even aware of giving them. One classic example is the case of Clever Hans, a horse in Germany at the turn of the century, which was said to be a genius. By pawing with its foot it could count, do arithmetic, spell out words, and even do square roots; right answers were, of course, rewarded with a tidbit. The owner, a retired schoolteacher, truly thought he had taught the horse to read, think, do math, and communicate. Indeed the animal would "answer" questions when the owner was not present. Many learned gentlemen traveled to Berlin to study Clever Hans and were convinced the horse was a genius. One psychologist eventually demonstrated that the horse was being cued somehow, in that if no one in the room knew the answer, the horse would paw indefinitely. It took much further investigation—over the protests of those who were convinced the horse really was a genius—to demonstrate that the cue to stop pawing was a minuscule lift of the owner's *or any qustioner's* head when the right number was reached, a movement originally exaggerated by a broad-brimmed hat the schoolteacher wore but by now so small that it was not only almost impossible to see (except by Clever Hans) but almost impossible to suppress by conscious effort. That was how the horse could tell when to stop pawing from watching people other than its owner. The Clever Hans phenomenon has now become the name for any

circumstance in which apparently amazing behavior, ranging from animal intelligence to psychic phenomena, is
actually unconsciously cued by some often-minute or faded
behavior of the experimenter that has become a conditioned stimulus for the subject.

Conditioned Aversive Stimuli

The one case where magnitude of a conditioned stimulus might seem to make a difference is in the traditional
training of domestic animals. Often the conditioned
stimulus—a tug on the reins, or on the leash, a nudge in
the horse's ribs—is a watered-down version of the original
unconditioned stimulus, the harsher pull or jerk or hard
kick that provoked an untrained response. So if the gentle
stimulus doesn't work, it seems as if you should get a
bigger response with a bigger stimulus. Efforts to put this
into practice lead to problems, however.

The learned signal and the primary stimulus are two
separate kinds of event, and novices tend to be unaware of
this. If they don't get a response to, say, a gentle pull,
they pull a little harder, then a little harder than that, all
quite futilely, as the horse or dog is pulling with equally
increasing force in the opposite direction.

Professionals tend to treat the cue and the use of
force separately; they give the conditioned stimulus, and if
it is not obeyed, they skip any gradations and immediately
elicit the behavior with an extremely strong aversive
stimulus—enough to "refresh his memory," as one horse
trainer puts it. This is the function of the choke chain used
in dog training. Properly taught, even a small person
using such a collar can give a quick jerk-and-release powerful enough to knock a Great Dane off its feet. With this
primary stimulus in reserve, one can quickly develop good
response to a very gentle tug; and as British trainer Bar-
bara Woodhouse points out, it is in the long run far kinder
than perpetually tugging and hauling on the poor beast's
neck at some intermediate and meaningless level of force.

Limited Holds

A very useful technique for getting prompt response to a conditioned stimulus is the limited hold. Let us say your subject has learned to offer a behavior in response to a conditioned stimulus but there is usually some gap in time between presentation of the stimulus and the subject's response. You call folks for supper and in due course they come, or you signal a halt and your elephant gradually slows to a stop.

If you wish, by using a limited hold, you can actually shape this interval downward until the behavior occurs as fast as is physically possible. You start by estimating the normal interval in which the behavior usually occurs; then you reinforce only behavior that occurs during that interval. Since living creatures are variable, some responses will fall outside the interval, and those no longer earn reinforcement. For example, if you serve supper a set time after calling, rather than waiting for stragglers, stragglers may get cold food or less choice of food.

When you set a time interval like this, and reinforce only within it, you will find that gradually all responses fall within that interval and no more are occurring outside it. Now you can tighten the screws again. Does it take fifteen minutes for the family to gather? Start serving twelve minutes after you call, or ten. How fast you tighten the screws is strictly a matter of judgment; as in any shaping procedure, you want to stay within the range where most of the behavior is occurring most of the time.

Animals and people have a very sharp time sense and will respond to limited-hold training with dramatic precision, but the trainer should not rely on guesswork. Use the clock, even a stopwatch, if you want limited-hold training to happen for you. On briefer behaviors, count to yourself, getting response time down from five beats to two, say. And of course, if you are working in a human situation, don't discuss what you are doing; you'll get nothing but arguments. Just do it and watch it work.

At Sea Life Park in the 1960s one of our most effective show highlights was a group of six little spinner dolphins performing several kinds of aerial acrobatics in unison. They did various leaps and whirls in response to underwater sound cues. Initially, when the cue went on, the leaps or spins, or whatever was called for, occurred raggedly and sporadically across a fifteen- to twenty-second period. By using a stopwatch and establishing a limited hold, we were able to crank down the performance interval to two and a half seconds. Every animal knew that in order to get a fish it had to hit the air and perform the right leap or spin within two and a half seconds of the time the cue went on. As a result, the animals poised themselves attentively near the underwater loudspeaker and when the cue went on the pool erupted in an explosion of whirling bodies in the air; it was quite spectacular. One day, while sitting among the audience, I was amused to overhear a professorial type, apparently a psychologist, firmly informing his companions that the only way we could be getting that kind of response was by electric shock.

Limited holds in real life are simply the amount of time you are willing to wait for a request or instruction to be carried out. Parents, bosses, and teachers who are consistent as to what they expect once the specific time interval has been established are usually regarded as fair and reliable to deal with, even if the limited hold—the "window" in time during which the behavior must occur in order to be reinforced—is quite brief.

Anticipation

A common flaw in stimulus-controlled behavior is anticipation: Once the cue has been learned, the subject is so eager to offer the behavior that it acts before the cue has actually been given. The expression describing this event comes from human anticipatory behavior in footraces: jumping the gun. People who anticipate cues or requests of others are generally perceived to be over-eager, fawning, or obsequious; it's an irritating habit, not a virtue.

Doberman pinschers sometimes run into trouble in obedience competitions. Although they are marvelously trainable dogs, they are so alert that they anticipate commands by the smallest of hints and often work before they have actually been told to, thus losing points. Anticipation is a common fault in calf-roping horses in rodeos. The cowboy and horse are supposed to wait behind a barrier for the calf to be given a head start, but the horse, excited, plunges off before the signal. The cowboy sometimes thinks he's got a real goer, but what he's really got is incompletely trained stimulus control. Another very common occurrence of anticipation is the "offsides" call in football. One player is so eager that he moves into the other team's territory before the signal to play is given, and the team must be penalized.

From a practical standpoint the way to cure anticipation is to use time-outs. If the subject anticipates the cue, and if that is undesirable, stop all activity. Give no cues and do nothing for one full minute. Every time the subject jumps the gun again, reset the clock. You are penalizing overeagerness by making it the cause of delay of the chance to work. This will effectively extinguish anticipating a command when rebuke, punishment, or repetition might have no effect at all.

Stimuli as Reinforcers: Behavior Chains

Once a conditioned stimulus is established, an interesting thing happens: It becomes a reinforcer. Think of the recess bell in school. The recess bell is a signal, a conditioned stimulus, meaning "You're excused, go out and play." And yet it is perceived as a reinforcer—children are glad to hear it, and if they could do something to make it ring sooner, they would. Now imagine a recess bell that does not ring unless the classroom is quiet. Around recess time you would get some very quiet classrooms.

A conditioned stimulus signals the opportunity for reinforcement, so it becomes a desirable event. A desirable event is in itself a reinforcer. That means that you can actually reinforce a behavior by presenting the conditioned stimulus for another behavior. For example: If I reward my cat with a tidbit for coming to me when I say "Come," and she learns this and does it, and if I then say "Come" and reinforce her for doing so each time I happen to see her sitting on the mantelpiece, it will soon happen that the cat, wanting a tidbit, will be found on the mantelpiece. (From her standpoint, remember, she is training me; she has found a way to get me to say "Come.") Now suppose I teach her to jump to the mantel when I point to it, using either food or "Come" as the reinforcer; and then I point to the mantel whenever: (a) I know she is hungry, and (b) she happens to roll on her back . . .

I have trained a behavior chain.

Behavior chains are very common. We often do long series of connected behaviors in real life, behaviors involving many known steps—carpentry and housework come to mind—and we expect our animals to do the same: "Come," "Sit," "Down," "Heel," and so on at length, with no obvious reinforcement. These long strings of behavior are behavior chains. Unlike simple long-duration behaviors—do this for an hour, do this a hundred times—they can be maintained comfortably, without deterioration or delayed starts, because each behavior is actually reinforced by the signal or opportunity to perform the next behavior, until the final reinforcement of a job completed.

Behavior chains break down, and the behavior goes to pieces, however, if there are unlearned behaviors in the chain, or behaviors that have not been brought under stimulus control. You can't reinforce the subject with a cue if it doesn't recognize the cue, or if it cannot accomplish what the cue indicates. This means that behavior chains should always be trained *backward*. Start with the last behavior in the chain; make sure it has been learned and that the signal to begin it is recognized; then train the

who wants his martinis (or his joint or his beer) right now, and his dinner shortly thereafter. The crabbier he is, the faster his wife rushes about to provide the necessaries, right? What is she actually reinforcing?

Crabbiness.

A cheerful demeanor, no speeding up of the supplies, and no hand wringing and upset on the spouse's part can do a lot to eliminate the usefulness to the crabby one of any display of moodiness or temper. On the other hand withdrawing into icy silence or screaming back or punishing would all be results, and consequently might be reinforcing.

By ignoring the behavior without ignoring the person, you can arrange for many disagreeable displays to extinguish by themselves because there is no result, good or bad. The behavior has become unproductive. Hostility requires a huge amount of energy, and if it doesn't work it is usually quickly abandoned.

Many behaviors are temporarily limited in themselves. When children or dogs or horses are first let out of doors after a period of confinement and inactivity, they crave to run and play. If you try to control this, you may have to exert quite a lot of effort. It's often easier just to let them run around for a while, until the behavior extinguishes by itself, before you ask for disciplined behavior or start to train them. Horse trainers call this "getting the bugs out." A wise horse trainer may turn a young horse loose in the ring for a few minutes, to kick and buck and run around, before saddling it and making it get to work. Calisthenics before drill-team or football practice serve somewhat the same purpose. In addition to getting the muscles moving, which reduces the chance of strains and injuries, these "gross motor activities" sop up some of the loose energy, so that romping and horseplay extinguish and the troops or players can become more attentive to the training process.

Habituation is a way to eliminate unconditioned responses. If a subject is exposed to an aversive stimulus that it cannot escape or avoid, and which nothing it does has any effect on, eventually its avoidance responses will extinguish. It will stop reacting to the stimulus, pay no attention, and apparently become unaware of it. This is called habituation. In my New York apartment I found the street noise unbearable at first, but eventually, like most New Yorkers, I learned to sleep through the sirens, yelling, garbage trucks, even car crashes. I became habituated. Police horses are sometimes trained by tying them down on the ground and then subjecting them to all kinds of harmless but alarming events, such as opening umbrellas, flapping papers, being tapped all over with rattling tin cans, and so on. The horses, unable to budge, become so habituated to startling sights and sounds that they remain unflappable no matter what events the city streets have to offer.

Method 5: Train an Incompatible Behavior

Here come the good fairies: the positive methods for getting rid of unwanted behavior.

One elegant method is to train the subject to perform another behavior physically incompatible with the one you don't want.

For example, some people do not like to have dogs begging at the dining-room table. I hate it myself—there is nothing more likely to curb my appetite than doggy breath, sad-dog eyes, and a heavy paw on my knee just as I am lifting a piece of steak to my mouth.

A Method 1 solution is to put the dog outside or shut it in another room during mealtimes. But it is also possible to control begging by training an incompatible behavior—for example, to train a dog to lie in the dining-room doorway when people are eating. First you train the dog to lie down, thereby bringing the behavior under stimulus control. You can then make the dog "Go lie down" elsewhere during meals. You reward this behavior with food when the plates are cleared. Going away and lying down is

Samples of Method 4: Extinction

Method 4 is not useful for getting rid of well-learned, self-rewarding behavior patterns. It is good, however, for whining, sulking, or teasing. Even small children can learn—and are gratified to discover—that they can stop older children from teasing them merely by not reacting in any way, good or bad.

Behavior	Approach
Roommate leaves dirty laundry all over the place.	Wait for him or her to grow up.
Dog in yard barks all night.	This behavior is self-reinforcing and seldom extinguishes spontaneously.
Kids too noisy in the car.	A certain amount of noise is natural and harmless; let it be, they'll get tired of it.
Spouse habitually comes home in a bad mood.	See to it that his or her harsh words have no results, either good or bad.
Faulty tennis swing.	Work on other strokes, footwork, and so on, and try to let specific error die down from lack of concentrating on it.
Shirking or lazy employee.	If the misbehavior is a way of getting attention, remove the attention; shirking, however, may be self-reinforcing.

Behavior	*Approach*
Hating to write thank-you notes.	This behavior generally extinguishes with age. Life becomes so full of onerous chores such as paying bills and doing taxes that mere thank-you notes become relaxation by comparison.
Cat gets on the kitchen table.	Ignore the behavior. It will not go away, but you may succeed in extinguishing your own objections to cat hair in your food.
Surly bus driver is rude to you and makes you mad.	Ignore the driver, pay your fare, and forget it.
An adult offspring who you think should be self-sufficient wants to move back in with you.	Accept it as a temporary measure and expect that the adult child will move out as soon as finances improve or the present crisis is over.

incompatible with begging at the table; a dog cannot physically be two places at once, and so begging is eliminated.

I once saw a symphony conductor hit on a brilliant use of an incompatible behavior during an opera rehearsal. The whole chorus suddenly fell out of synchrony with the orchestra. It seemed they had memorized one measure of music a beat short. Having identified the problem, the conductor looked for an "s" in the lyrics of that measure, found one, and told the chorus to stress that "s": "The king'sssss coming." It made a funny buzzing sound, but it was incompatible with rushing through the measure too fast and solved the problem.

My own first use of Method 5 was in the handling of a potentially very serious dolphin problem. At Sea Life Park we at one time had three kinds of performers in the outdoor show: a group of six dainty little spinner dolphins, a huge female bottlenose named Apo, and a pretty Hawaiian girl who swam and played with the spinner dolphins during part of the show. Contrary to popular opinion, dolphins are not always friendly, and bottlenoses in particular are apt to bully and tease. Apo, the six-hundred-pound bottlenose, took to harassing the swimmer when she got in the water, dashing under her and boosting her into the air, or slapping her on the head with her tail flukes. It terrified the girl, and it was indeed very dangerous.

We did not want to take Apo out of the show, since her leaps and flips made her its star. We started constructing a pen in which she could be shut during the swimmer's performance—a Method 1 solution—but meanwhile we trained an incompatible behavior. We got Apo to press on an underwater lever, at the pool's edge, in return for fish rewards.

Apo enthusiastically learned to press the lever repeatedly for each fish; she even took to defending her lever from other dolphins. And during shows a trainer put Apo's lever in the pool and reinforced lever pressing whenever the swimmer was out in mid-water playing with the spinners. Apo could not press her lever and simultaneously be in the middle of the pool beating up the swimmer; the two behaviors were incompatible. Fortunately Apo preferred lever pressing to swimmer harassment, so the behavior was eliminated (the swimmer, however, never quite trusted this magic and calmed down completely only when Apo was back safely behind bars).

Training an incompatible behavior is a good way to attack a faulty tennis swing or any other muscular pattern that has been learned wrong. Muscles "learn" slowly but well; once something has become part of your movement patterns it is hard to unlearn. (Piano lessons were frustrating to me as a child because it seemed in every piece my fingers would learn one note wrong and stumble in the same place every time.) One way to deal with this is to train an incompatible behavior. Using a tennis swing as an example, first take the movement apart in your mind—posture, position, footwork, start, middle, and end—and go very slowly through each portion of the movement, or many times through just one portion if necessary. Train a completely different swing, a set of new motions. When the muscles begin to learn the new pattern, you can put it together and speed it up.

When you start using it in playing time, at full speed, you must pay absolutely no attention at first to where the ball goes; just practice the movement pattern. Now you should have two swings—the old faulty one and the new one. The two are incompatible; you cannot make two swings at once. But while you may never get rid of the old pattern completely, you can reduce it to a minimum by replacing it with the new one. Once that pattern has become a muscle habit, you can concentrate again on where the ball goes. And presumably, with a better swing, the ball will behave better too. (This is also how I could have tackled my piano-lesson problem.)

Training an incompatible behavior is quite useful in modifying your own behavior, especially when dealing with emotional states such as grief, anxiety, and loneliness. Some behaviors are totally incompatible with self-pity: dancing, choral singing, or any highly kinetic motor activity, even running. You cannot engage in them and wallow in misery simultaneously. Feeling awful? Try Method 5.

Method 6: Put the Behavior on Cue

This one's a dilly. It works in some circumstances when nothing else will suffice.

It is an axiom of learning theory that when a behavior is brought under stimulus control—that is, when the organism learns to offer the behavior in response to some kind of cue and only then—the behavior tends to extinguish in the absence of the cue. You can use this natural law to

Samples of Method 5: Train an Incompatible Behavior

Sensible people often employ this method. Singing and playing games in the car relieves parents as well as children from boredom. Diversion, distraction, and pleasant occupations are good alternatives during many tense moments.

Behavior	*Approach*
Roommate leaves dirty laundry all over the place.	Buy a laundry hamper and reward roommate for placing laundry in it. Wash laundry together, making it a social occasion, when hamper is full. Laundry care is incompatible with laundry neglect.
Dog in yard barks all night.	Train it to lie down on command; dogs, like most of us, seldom bark lying down. Yell command out window or rig intercom to doghouse. Reward with praise.
Kids too noisy in the car.	Sing songs, tell stories, play games: "Ghost," "I Spy with My Little Eye," "20 Questions," "Found a Peanut," and so on. Even three-year-olds can sing "Found a Peanut." Incompatible with squabbling and yelling.
Spouse habitually comes home in a bad mood.	Institute some pleasant activity on homecoming, incompatible with grouching, such as playing with the children, working on a hobby. Thirty minutes of total privacy is often good. Spouse may need time to unwind before switching to family life.

Behavior	Approach
Faulty tennis swing.	Train an alternative tennis swing from scratch (see text).
Shirking or lazy employee.	Order him or her to work quicker or harder on a specific task; watch, and praise the job on completion.
Hating to write thank-you notes.	Train some replacement behavior: If someone sends you a check, write a few grateful words on the back as you endorse it—the bank will take care of the rest. For other kinds of presents, call the sender that very night and say thank you. Then you will never have to write a letter.
Cat gets on the kitchen table.	Train the cat to sit on a kitchen chair for petting and food reward. An eager or hungry cat may hit that chair so hard it slides halfway across the kitchen, but still the cat is where you want it, not on the table.
Surly bus driver is rude to you and makes you mad.	Respond to snarls or bullying with eye contact, a civil smile, and an appropriate social remark —"Good morning"—or, if the driver is really scolding you, "Thank you, that's quite all right." This baffling misresponse sometimes elicits courtesy in return.
An adult offspring who you think should be self-sufficient wants to move back in with you.	Help him or her to find another place to live, even if you have to pay for it at first.

get rid of all kinds of things you don't want, simply by bringing the behavior under the control of a cue . . . and then never giving the cue.

I first discovered the use of this elegant method while training a dolphin to wear blindfolds. We wanted to give a demonstration of dolphin sonar, or echolocation, in our public shows at Sea Life Park. I intended to train a male bottlenose dolphin named Makua to wear rubber suction cups over his eyes, and then, temporarily blinded, to locate and retrieve objects underwater using his echolocation system. The behavior has become a standard item in oceanarium shows nowadays.

The blindfolds didn't hurt Makua, but he didn't care for them. By and by, when he saw the suction cups in my hands, he took to sinking to the bottom of the tank and staying there. He would lie there for up to five minutes at a time, waving his tail gently and watching me up through the water with a "Gotcha!" look in his eye.

I judged it would be unprofitable to try to scare or poke him up to the surface, and foolish to bribe or lure him. So one day, when he sank on me, I rewarded him with the whistle and a bunch of fish. Makua emitted a "surprise bubble"—a basketball-sized sphere of air which, in the dolphin world, means "Huh?"—and came up and ate his fish. Soon he was sinking on purpose, to earn reinforcement.

Then I introduced an underwater sound as a cue and reinforced him only for sinking on cue. Sure enough, he stopped sinking in the absence of the cue. Sinking was never a problem again; when I went back to blindfold training, he accepted his blindfolds like a trouper.

I have also used this method to calm down noisy kids in the car. If you are on your way to someplace wonderful—the circus, say—the children may be noisy because they are excited, too excited to be amenable to Method 5, playing games and singing songs. And on a happy occasion you don't want to use Method 3, negative reinforcement, by pulling over and stopping the car. Now Method 6 is

Samples of Method 6: Put the Behavior on Cue

It doesn't seem logical that this method would work, but it can be startlingly effective, and sometimes almost an instantaneous cure.

Behavior	Approach
Roommate leaves dirty laundry all over the place.	Have a laundry fight. See how big a mess you can both make in ten minutes. (Effective; sometimes the untidy person, seeing what a big mess looks like, is then able to recognize and tidy up smaller messes—one shirt, two socks—that may still bother you but were previously not perceived as messy by the roommate.)
Dog in yard barks all night.	Train the dog to bark on command "Speak!" for a food reward. In the absence of the command, no point in barking.
Kids too noisy in the car.	Put noisemaking under stimulus control (see text).
Spouse habitually comes home in a bad mood.	Set a time and a signal for grouching; sit down for ten minutes, say, starting at 5 P.M. During that period reinforce all complaining with your full attention and sympathy. Ignore complaining before and after.

Behavior	Approach
Faulty tennis swing.	If you told yourself to hit the ball wrong, and learned to do it on purpose, would the fault tend to extinguish when you did not give the command? It might.
Shirking or lazy employee.	Order up goof-off time. This was an amazingly effective technique used by the president of an ad agency where I once worked.
Hating to write thank-you notes.	Buy a memo pad, notepaper, stamps, a pen, an address book, and a red box. Put the supplies inside the box. When you get a present, write the donor's name on the memo pad, put it on the box, put the red box on your pillow or dinner plate, and don't sleep or eat until you've obeyed the cue of the box and written the letter and sealed, stamped, and mailed it.
Cat gets on the kitchen table.	Train it to jump up on the table on cue and also to jump down on cue (this impresses guests). You can then shape the length of time it has to wait for the cue (all day, eventually).
Surly bus driver is rude to you and makes you mad.	Putting this behavior on cue is not recommended.

Behavior	*Approach*
An adult offspring who you think should be self-sufficient wants to move back in with you.	As soon as adult children leave home for good, invite them back for visits, making it clear that they should come only by your invitation. Then don't invite them to move in.

useful: Bring the behavior under stimulus control. "Okay, everybody make as much noise as you possibly can, starting NOW!" (You make noise, too.) This is a lot of fun for about thirty seconds, and then it palls. Two or three repetitions is usually more than enough to ensure reasonable quiet for the rest of the ride. You could say that being noisy on cue takes the fun out of it; or you could say that behavior occurring under stimulus control tends to extinguish in the absence of the stimulus.

Deborah Skinner, daughter of psychologist B. F. Skinner, passed on to me a splendid use of Method 6 to control dogs crying at the door. She had a small dog which, when shut outside, would bark and whine at the back door instead of going off and relieving itself. Deborah made a small cardboard disk, one side black and the other white, that she hung on the outside door handle. When the black side was out, no amount of yapping would make the people inside open the door. When the white side was out, the dog would be let in. The dog quickly learned not to bother trying to get back in on the black cue. When Deborah judged that an appropriate amount of time had passed she would open the door a crack, turn the cue around, then let the dog in as soon as it asked.

I tried Deborah's doorknob cue when my daughter acquired a toy poodle puppy. Peter was a very small dog, barely six inches high at two months, and it really was not safe to let him run around loose even indoors with no one to watch him. When I was busy and Gale was at school, I shut him in Gale's room, with food, water, newspapers, and a blanket.

Of course when he was shut up alone he made a terrible racket. I decided to try Deborah's trick by providing a signal for when barking would and would not be responded to. I grabbed the nearest thing—a small towel— and hung it on the inside doorknob. When the towel was there, no amount of yapping would produce results. When the towel was removed, the puppy's calls for company and freedom would be answered.

The puppy caught on right away and gave up agitating when the towel was on the doorknob. The only thing I had to remember in order to maintain the behavior was not to just let the puppy out when I felt like doing so, but to open the door, remove the towel, close the door, wait till the puppy barked, and *then* let him out, thus keeping the barking behavior under stimulus control (in this case, "no towel" being the signal for barking-will-be-rewarded), and thus also keeping all other barking extinguished.

It worked splendidly—for three days. Then one morning Peter's noisy demands were suddenly heard anew. I opened the door and discovered that he had figured out how to leap up, with all his tiny might, and jerk the towel off the doorknob. Once the towel was on the floor, he felt perfectly free to call for release.

Method 7: Shape the Absence of the Behavior

This is a useful technique in cases where you don't have anything particular that you wish the subject to do, just that you want him to stop what he is doing. Example: complaining, guilt-engendering phone calls from relatives whom you like and don't wish to hurt by Method 1, hanging up, or by Methods 2 or 3, scolding or ridicule.

Animal psychologist Harry Frank, who was socializing wolf pups by bringing them into the house for daily visits, decided to reinforce, with petting and attention, anything that was not in the category of destroying property. It

Samples of Method 7: Shape the Absence of Unwanted Behaviors

This takes some conscious effort over a period of time, but is often the best way to change deeply ingrained behavior.

Behavior	*Approach*
Roommate leaves dirty laundry all over the place.	Buy beer or invite over members of the opposite sex whenever quarters are tidy or roommate does the laundry.
Dog in yard barks all night.	Go out and reward him now and then at night when he has been quiet for ten, twenty minutes, an hour, and so on.
Kids too noisy in the car.	Wait for a quiet time and then say "You all have been so quiet today that I'm going to stop at McDonald's." (Say this right near McDonald's so you can keep your promise promptly, before they get noisy again!)
Spouse habitually comes home in a bad mood.	Think up some good reinforcements and surprise him or her with them whenever the mood does happen to be pleasant.
Faulty tennis swing.	Ignore bad shots, and praise yourself for good ones. (This *really* works.)
Shirking or lazy employee.	Praise the hell out of him for any job actually done satisfactorily. (You do not have to keep

Behavior	*Approach*
	this up for a lifetime, just long enough to establish the new trend.)
Hating to write thank-you notes.	Treat yourself to a movie any time you get a present and promptly write and mail the thank-you note.
Cat gets on the kitchen table.	Rewarding the cat for periods of staying off the table is practical only if you keep the kitchen door closed when you're not home so the cat can't indulge in behavior by itself.
Surly bus driver is rude to you and makes you mad.	If you run into the same bus driver on your route every day, a pleasant good morning when he or she is not being rude should lead to improvement in a week or two.
An adult offspring who you think should be self-sufficient wants to move back in with you.	Reinforce adult children for living away from home when they are doing so. Don't criticize their housekeeping, choice of apartment, decor, or taste in friends, or they may decide you're right, your house is a better place to live.

turned out that about the only pastime in a human household that did not involve the pups' chewing up couches, telephone wires, rugs, and so on was lying on the bed; in due course evenings were passed peacefully with Harry, his wife, and three increasingly large young wolves lying on the family bed, watching the ten o'clock news. Method 7.

I used Method 7 to change my mother's behavior on the telephone. An invalid for some years, my mother lived in a nursing home. I visited her when I could, but most of our communication took place on the telephone. For years, these phone calls were a trouble to me. The conversations were usually, and sometimes exclusively, concerned with my mother's problems—pain, loneliness, lack of money. Real problems I was powerless to mitigate. Her complaints would turn to tears, and tears to accusations—accusations that made me angry. The exchanges were unpleasant, to the extent that I tended to duck the phone calls.

It occurred to me that there might be a better way. I began concentrating on my own behavior during these phone calls. I used Method 4 and Method 7. I deliberately let her complaints and tears extinguish—Method 4—by saying "Ah," and "Hmm," and "Well, well." No real results, good or bad. I did not hang up, or attack; I let nothing happen. I then reinforced anything and everything that was not a complaint: queries about my children, news from the nursing home, discussion of weather, or books, or friends. These remarks I responded to with enthusiasm. Method 7.

To my astonishment, after twenty years of conflict, within two months the proportion of tears and distress to chat and laughter in our weekly phone calls became reversed. At the start of the phone calls my mother's worries—"Have you mailed a check? Did you talk to the doctor? Would you call my social worker?"—turned into simple requests instead of reiterated grievances. Now the rest of the time became filled with gossip, reminiscing, and jokes.

My mother had been in her youth, and became again, a fascinating, witty woman. For the remaining years of her life I really loved talking to her, in person and on the phone.

"Isn't that awfully manipulative?" a psychiatrist friend once asked. Sure. What was happening before to me was awfully manipulative, too. Perhaps some therapist might have persuaded me to deal differently with my mother, or she with me, but perhaps not. How much simpler it seemed to have a clear-cut Method 7 goal. What are you actually reinforcing? Anything but what you don't want.

Method 8: Change the Motivation

Eliminating the motivation for a behavior is often the kindliest and most effective method of all. The person who has enough to eat is not going to steal a loaf of bread.

A common sight I always wince at is the mother whose small child is having a tantrum in the supermarket and who is jerking on the kid's arm to make it hush up. Of course one can empathize—the tantrum is embarrassing, and jerking is a surreptitious way to shock the child into silence, less conspicuous than yelling or smacking (it's also a good way to dislocate a little child's elbow or shoulder, as any orthopedic surgeon can tell you). The problem is usually that the child is hungry, and the sight and smell of all that food is too much for it. Very few young mothers have someone to leave the kids with while they market, and working mothers especially often have to market right before dinnertime, when they themselves are tired and hungry and hence irritable.

The solution is to feed the kids before or while going to the market; any sort of junk food would be preferable to the distressing scenes that upset child, mother, checkout clerks, and everyone else within range.

Some behaviors are self-reinforcing—that is, the very enactment of the behavior is a reinforcement. Gum chewing, smoking, and thumb sucking are examples. The best

145

way to get rid of these behaviors in yourself or another is to change the motivation. I gave up chewing gum as a child because an aunt told me it made girls look cheap, and not looking "cheap" was a lot more important to me than the pleasure of chewing gum. Smokers quit when their motives for smoking are met in other ways or when motivation to stop—fear of cancer, say—outweighs the reinforcement of smoking. Thumb sucking stops when a child's level of confidence is high enough so that he or she no longer needs the self-comforting.

To change motivation, one needs to make an accurate estimate of what the motivation is, and we are often very incompetent at that. We love to jump to conclusions: "She hates my guts," "The boss has it in for me," "That kid is just no damned good." Often we don't even understand our own motivations. The whole profession of psychology and psychiatry has arisen in part for that reason.

Even if we have no unhealthy motivations ourselves, we pay a big penalty for this popular awareness of hidden motivation, especially when we must rely on the medical professions. Physical problems, if not blatantly obvious, are all too often assumed to be emotional in origin and are treated as such, without further examination for a real physical cause. I've seen a businessman treated with amphetamines so he would stop "feeling" exhausted, when in fact he *was* exhausted from overwork. In a West Coast city, a woman recently was diagnosed as neurotic and treated with tranquilizers by half a dozen doctors who apparently saw no physical reason for her symptoms. She nearly ended up in a mental hospital before the seventh doctor discovered she was not malingering but in fact was slowly dying of carbon monoxide poisoning due to a leaky furnace in her home. I myself had some doctor I'd never seen before give me a scolding and a prescription for tranquilizers when what was wrong—and I'd told him I thought so—was an incipient case of the mumps.

Sometimes, of course, the motive really consists of a need for reassurance, and therefore (if the dispenser of relief is perceived as a powerful and believable person) a tranquilizer or even a sugar pill, or placebo, can calm the spirit, lower the blood pressure, and ease symptoms. Holy water and a blessing can do it, too, if you believe they will. The so-called placebo effect also probably helps to keep witch doctors in business. I see nothing wrong with that. The motivation is a need for reassurance, a very genuine need. The trick in any circumstance is to identify the motivation, rather than just jump to conclusions. One way to do that is to notice what actually helps change the behavior and what doesn't.

The message: If you or a friend has a puzzling behavioral problem, think hard about possible motivations. Never forget the possibility of a cause such as hunger, illness, loneliness, or fear. If it is possible to eliminate the underlying cause, and thus eliminate or change the motivation, you've got it made.

Motivation and Deprivation

Motivation is a huge subject to which scientists have devoted lifetimes of study. By and large it lies outside the scope of this book, but because it has been necessary to discuss motivation as it relates to undesirable behavior, perhaps this is the place to discuss a training device sometimes used to heighten motivation: deprivation. The theory is if an animal is working for positive reinforcement, the more it needs that reinforcement the harder and more reliably it will work. Laboratory rats and pigeons are often conditioned with food reinforcement. To heighten their motivation, they are fed less food than they would eat on their own. It is customary to give them just enough to keep them at 85 percent of normal body weight. This is called food deprivation.

Deprivation has become such a standard technique in experimental psychology that when I started training I assumed it was probably a necessity in working with rats and pigeons. Of course we did not use deprivation with dolphins. Our dolphins were given all they would eat whether they'd earned it or not at the end of each day, since dolphins that do not get enough to eat often become sick and die.

It did occur to me in those days that I was using food and social reinforcement with ponies and children, quite successfully, without first having to reduce the baseline supply of love or nourishment to get results. Perhaps food deprivation was necessary only with simpler organisms, such as rats and pigeons? Yet our Sea Life Park trainers were shaping behavior with food reinforcement in pigs, chickens, penguins, even fish and octopi, and no one ever dreamed of making the poor things extra-hungry first.

I still thought deprivation must be necessary in some kinds of training, since it is so widely used . . . until I ran into Dave Butcher's sea lions. I had never worked with sea lions myself, and my cursory impression was that they worked only for fish, and that they were antisocial and bit trainers. I also thought that only young animals were used for training. All the working animals I had ever seen were comparatively small, between one hundred and two hundred pounds, and I knew that sea lions in the wild get quite large. Dave Butcher, director of training for Sea World in Florida, showed me more than I'd imagined possible. His sea lions worked for social and tactile reinforcements as well as fish, and of course for conditioned reinforcers and on variable schedules as well. Consequently they did not have to be kept hungry in order to make them perform; during and after the day's performances the sea lions could have all the fish they wanted. One result was that the sea lions were not snarly and crabby, as any hungry animal might be. They were friendly to those humans they knew and enjoyed being touched. I was astonished to see trainers on their lunch hour sunbathing in a pile with their sea lions, each young man resting against the ample flank of one sea lion, with the head of another sea lion in his lap. Another result of the discontinuance of food deprivation was that these sea lions grew

Samples of Method 8: Change the Motivation

If you can find a way to do it, this method always works and is the best of all.

Behavior	*Approach*
Roommate leaves dirty laundry all over the place.	Hire a maid or housekeeper to tidy up and do laundry, so neither you nor the roommate has to cope. This may be the best solution if you are married to this roommate and you both work. Or the messy person could shape the tidy one to be more casual.
Dog in yard barks all night.	Barking dogs are lonely, frightened, and bored. Give exercise and attention by day so dog is tired and sleepy at night, or provide another dog to sleep with at night for company.
Kids too noisy in the car.	Escalation of noise and conflict is often due to hunger and fatigue. Provide juice, fruit, and cookies, and pillows for comfortable lounging, on home-from-school trips. On long journeys, all of the above plus ten minutes per hour of stopping and running around outdoors (good for parents too).
Spouse habitually comes home in a bad mood.	Encourage a job change. Feed cheese and crackers or a cup of hot soup right at the door if hunger and fatigue are the mo-

149

Behavior	Approach
	tivation. If stress is the problem, a drink or two may well be an appropriate solution.
Faulty tennis swing.	Stop trying to beat the world by winning on the tennis court. Play for fun. (Not applicable to world-class tennis players—or is it?)
Shirking or lazy employee.	Pay for work done, not for hours put in. Task-oriented payment is often very effective with nonWestern employees. It's the barn-raising principle; everyone works like mad until the known task is completed, and then everyone can leave. Hollywood movies are made this way.
Hating to write thank-you notes.	We dislike this task because it is a behavior chain (see Method 6) and therefore hard to start, especially since there is no good reinforcement at the end (we already have the present!). We also sometimes put it off because we think we have to write a good, clever, or perfect letter. Not true: All the recipient needs to know is that you are grateful for his or her symbol of affection. Fancy words in a thank-you note are no more important than fancy penmanship on a check: On-time delivery is what counts.

Behavior	*Approach*
Cat gets on the kitchen table.	Why do cats get on the table? 1) to look for food, so put the food away; 2) cats like to lounge in a high place where they can see what's going on. Arrange a shelf or a pedestal higher than the tabletop, close enough so you can pet the cat, and offering a good view of the kitchen, and the cat may well prefer it.
Surly bus driver is rude to you and makes you mad.	Avoid being snarled at on buses by doing *your* job: have your change ready, know your destination, don't block the aisle, don't mumble questions, try to be sympathetic about traffic tie-ups, and so on. Bus drivers get crabby because bus riders can be such a pain.
An adult offspring who you think should be self-sufficient wants to move back in with you.	Adults with friends, self-esteem, a purpose in life, some kind of work, and a roof over their heads usually don't want to live with or on their parents. Help your kids find the first three as they are growing up, and they'll usually take care of the job and the roof on their own. Then you can all stay friends.

. . . and grew! Most trained sea lions in the past, Dave speculated, were small not because of youth but because they were stunted. Sea World's performers weigh six, seven, eight hundred pounds. They are very active, not a bit obese, but they are huge, as nature intended. And they work hard. The five or more daily shows are marvelous.

It's my suspicion now that trying to increase motivation by using deprivation of any sort is not only unnecessary but deleterious. Reducing the normal levels of food, attention, company, or anything else a subject likes or needs before training begins—and solely in order to make the reinforcement more powerful by making the subject more needful—is just a poor excuse for bad training. Maybe it has to be used in the laboratory, but in the real world it is good training that creates high motivation, not the other way around.

Getting Rid of Complicated Problems

In the tables in this chapter I have shown how each of the eight methods might be applied to specific behavioral problems. For some problems there are one or two solutions that are obviously best. For the dog that barks in the night from fear and loneliness, bringing the dog inside or providing it with a companion will usually ensure that it barks only when genuinely alarmed. For other problems, different methods are appropriate at different times. One can keep children from being too noisy in the car in several ways, depending on the circumstances.

There are other behavioral problems, however, that arise from multiple motives, become firmly entrenched, and are not controllable by any single method—stress symptoms such as nail biting, bad habits such as chronic lateness, addictive behaviors such as smoking. These behaviors can be reduced or eliminated by calculated use of the eight methods, but it may take a combination of several methods to bring the behavior to a halt (and again, I am talking about behavioral problems only in reasonably normal subjects, not in mentally ill or damaged subjects).

Let's look at some examples of problems requiring multiple-method approaches.

Biting Your Nails

Nail biting is both a symptom of stress and a diversion that tends to relieve tension momentarily. In animals such activity is called displacement behavior. A dog in a situation of tension—for instance when being coaxed over to be petted by a stranger—may suddenly sit down and scratch itself. Two horses threatening each other in a dominance conflict may suddenly go through the motions of grazing. Displacement behavior very often consists of self-grooming activities. In animals under conditions of confinement, the behavior may be carried out so repetitiously that it leads to self-mutilation. Birds preen their feathers until they have plucked themselves bare; cats lick a paw until they have created an open wound. Nail biting (and hair pulling, scratching, and other grooming behaviors) can be carried to this extreme in people, and yet even pain does not stop the behavior.

Because the behavior does indeed distract one from stress momentarily, it becomes self-reinforcing and thus very hard to get rid of. In fact, it becomes a habit and can occur even when there is no stress around. Sometimes Method 4 works—extinction. The habit fades away as one grows older and more confident. But that can take years. Method 1—making nail biting impossible by, say, wearing gloves—and Method 2—punishment by guilt or scoldings—will not teach the nail biter an alternative behavior. Method 3, negative reinforcement—painting the fingernails with something bad-tasting perhaps—is effective only if the habit is fading away anyway (this goes for thumb sucking too).

If you have this habit, the best way to get rid of it is probably to use a combination of all four of the positive methods. First, using Method 5, an incompatible behavior, learn to observe yourself starting to nail-bite, and every time your hand drifts toward your mouth, jump up and do something else. Take four deep breaths. Drink a glass of water. Hop up and down. Stretch. You cannot be nail biting and doing these things at the same time (and all are, in themselves, tension relievers).

Meanwhile, work on Method 8, changing the motivation. Reduce the overall stress in your life. Share your worries with others, who may in fact have solutions. Get more physical exercise, which usually enables one to face problems more easily. You can also shape the absence of behavior (Method 7) by rewarding yourself with a ring or a good manicure as soon as one and then another nail grows enough to be visible (even if you had to bandage a finger to get there at first). And you might also try psychologist Jennifer James's excellent suggestion for putting the behavior on cue: All day long, every time you find yourself starting to bite your nails, write down what is bothering you at the moment. Then every evening sit down at a specific time and bite your nails continuously for twenty minutes while worrying over everything on your list. In due course, you should be able to shape the nail-biting time down to zero, especially if you combine this effort with the other methods above.

Chronic Lateness

People who lead complex, demanding lives sometimes get to places late because they have too much to do and have to try to cram it all in somehow—working mothers, people in new and fast-growing businesses, some doctors, and so on. Other people tend to be late as a general rule, whether they are busy or not. Since some of the world's busiest people are impeccably punctual, we have to suspect that some of the people who are often late are subconsciously choosing to be so.

One would think that tardiness would carry its own

downfall, in the form of negative reinforcement—you miss half the movie, the party is almost over, the person you kept waiting is furious. But these are apt to be punishments, not negative reinforcements, in that they occur after the behavior that needs to be changed, which is *not* arriving late but instead failing to start off soon enough to get where you're going on time. And habitually late people generally have marvelous excuses prepared, for which they are pleasantly reinforced with forgiveness (which develops their excuse-making skills and in fact reinforces late arriving).

The fastest way to conquer being late is Method 8, changing the motivation. People have many reasons for being late. One is fear: You don't want to be in school, so you dawdle. Another is a bid for sympathy: "Poor little me, I have been saddled with so many responsibilities that I cannot meet my commitments." There is hostile lateness—when you secretly do not wish to be with those people at all—and show-off lateness, when you make it obvious that you have much more important things to do with your time than show up here.

It really doesn't matter what the particular motives are in a given case. To stop being late all one has to do is change the motivation by deciding that in all circumstances being on time is going to have first priority over any other consideration. Presto! You will never have to run for a plane or miss an appointment again. As a lifelong latecomer, that's how I cured myself. Having made the decision that promptness was now of major importance, I found that answers came automatically to such questions as "Do I have time to get my hair done before the committee meeting?" or "Can I squeeze in one more errand before the dentist?" or "Do I have to leave for the airport now?" The answers are always no, no, and yes. Once in a while I still slip up, but by and large choosing to be on time has made my life enormously easier, and that of family, friends, and colleagues as well.

If changing the motivation is not enough for you, you

could add Method 5, training an incompatible behavior, by aiming at getting places early (bring a book). Or add Method 7, shaping the absence—reinforce yourself, and get your friends to reinforce you, for what in others might be normal but what in you takes special effort, absence of lateness. And try Method 6, putting lateness on cue. Choose some events to which you truly wish to be late, announce that you intend to be late, and then be late. Since behavior occurring on cue tends to extinguish in the absence of the signal, being deliberately late when it's safe to be so may help extinguish being "accidentally" or unconsciously late when you really should be on time.

Addictions

Addictions to ingested substances—cigarette smoke, alcohol, caffeine, drugs, and so on—have physical effects that tend to keep you hooked whatever you do and to give you nasty withdrawal symptoms if you must go without the substance. But there are huge behavior components to these addictions as well. Some people behave as if addicted, including suffering withdrawal symptoms, to relatively harmless substances such as tea, soda pop, and chocolate, or to pastimes such as running and eating. Some people can turn addictions on and off. Most smokers, for example, find that the urge to smoke hits as regularly as a clock and that they are frantic if they run out of cigarettes. But some Orthodox Jews can smoke heavily six days a week and then abstain completely on the Sabbath without a pang.

In addition to physical symptoms, most addictions provide temporary stress relief, so that they become displacement activities, which makes them doubly hard to eliminate. But because addictions have strong behavioral components, it is conceivable that any addiction problem can be tackled behaviorally by one or more of the eight methods with some possibility of good results.

Almost all addict-rehabilitation programs, from dry-out clinics to Synanon, rely heavily on Methods 1 and 8. The desired substance is made physically unavailable, and therapy is given to try to find some other source of satisfaction for the subject—increased self-esteem, insight, job skills, whatever—to change the motivation that provides the needfulness. Many treatments also rely on Method 2, punishment, usually by preaching about lapses and thus inducing guilt. I once went through a quit-smoking program, which was in fact very helpful, even though I frequently cheated. When I cheated—smoked someone else's cigarettes at a tense business meeting, for example—I felt dreadfully guilty; the next morning I would be practically ill with guilt. But that didn't stop me the next time; Methods 2 and 3, punishment and negative reinforcement, did not work very well for me. But they do for some. Weight-loss programs often emphasize not only public praise for losing pounds but shame in front of the group for gaining, and some people will work to avoid the possibility of that shame.

A lot of addictive behavior has elements of superstitious behavior. The action—eating, smoking, whatever—has accidentally gotten hooked to environmental cues that trigger the urge. A time of day makes you want a drink, the phone rings and you think of lighting up a cigarette, and so on. Systematic identification of all these cues, and extinction of the behavior by *not* doing it on each cue, one cue at a time, is a valuable Method 4 adjunct to getting rid of an addictive habit. This might mean something simple such as putting the ashtrays out of sight, or it might involve a whole change of scenery, a move to a new environment where nothing constitutes an old familiar trigger cue (cured heroin addicts are not likely to stay clean if they go right back to life on familiar streets).

Negative reinforcement has been touted as a behavioral method for controlling addiction. Alcoholics, for example, have been wired up and then given shocks while lifting a glass of liquor, and medicine exists that will make you vomit if you ingest alcohol. Like most negative reinforcements, these work well only if there is someone around to administer them, and preferably unpredictably.

Like most addictive behavior, alcohol dependency doesn't yield very easily to just one method. I think the way to tackle addictive behavior in yourself—and this is one situation where the subject may very well be the most effective trainer—is to study all eight methods and find some way, with the exception of punishment, to engage in frequent application of every single one.

5
Reinforcement in the Real World

Very early in this book, in discussing Skinnerian theory, I pointed out that Schopenhauer once said that every original idea is first ridiculed, then vigorously attacked, and finally taken for granted. I think there is a fourth step in the evolution of an idea: The idea is not only accepted, but understood, cherished, and put to work. This is what I see beginning to happen with positive reinforcement, especially among people who have grown up with Skinnerian concepts in the Zeitgeist, in the air around them—people, that is, who have been born since 1950. They take to positive reinforcement and shaping without fear or resistance, as children nowadays take to the computers that their parents may still shrink from. They share techniques with their elders, and they infect those around them with their enthusiasm. Let me give you some examples I find heartening.

Reinforcement in Sports

From my casual observations, the training of most team sports—pro football, for example—continues in the good old Neanderthal tradition: lots of deprivation, punishment, favoritism, and verbal and mental abuse. The training of individual sports, however, seems to be undergoing a revolution. In fact, it was a symptom of that revolution which prompted the writing of this book. At a dinner party in Westchester County, New York, I was seated next to my hostess's tennis pro, a nice young man from Australia. He said to me, "I hear you were a dolphin trainer. Do you know about Skinner and all that?"

"Yes."

"Well, tell me, where can I get a book about Skinner that will help me be a better tennis coach?"

I knew there was no such thing. Why there wasn't continues to be a mystery to me, but I set out to write one, and here it is. Meanwhile, I pondered the amazing fact that this person, and presumably many like him, knew exactly what was needed. It meant there are people out there who already have a grasp of reinforcement training and want to know more about it.

At that time I was living in New York City. Partly for relief from house-pent, sedentary city life, and partly from a trainer's curiosity, I began to take a few lessons in various kinds of physical activities ranging from name-brand exercise classes to squash, sailing, skiing (both downhill and cross-country), figure skating, and dance.

To my surprise only one of the instructors I worked under (the exercise-class teacher) relied on traditional brow-beating and ridicule to elicit behavior. All the rest used well-timed positive reinforcement and often very ingenious shaping procedures. This contrasted sharply with my earlier memories of physical instruction—ballet classes, riding lessons, gym classes at school and college—none of which I shined in, and all of which I feared as much as enjoyed. Ice skating, for example. I took figure-skating lessons as a child at a large and successful skating school. The instructor showed us what to do, and then we practiced and struggled until we could do it while the instructor corrected our posture and arm positions and exhorted us to try harder. I never could learn my "outside edges" —gliding in a circle to the left, say, with my weight on the outside edge of the left foot. Since that was preliminary to most of the figures, I didn't get very far.

Now I tried a few lessons at a modern skating school in New York, managed by an Olympic coach. The staff used exactly the same methods on adults as on children—no scolding or urging, just instant reinforcement for each accomplishment; and there was plenty of accomplishment. Every single thing a skater needs to know was broken down into easily managed shaping steps, starting with falling down and getting up again. Gliding on one foot? Easy: Shove off from the wall, feet parallel, gliding on two feet; lift one up, ever so briefly, put it down, then lift the other; then do it again, lift a little longer, and so on. In ten minutes the entire beginners' class, including the fat, the weak, the wobbly, the very young and the very old, were gliding on one foot with looks of wild astonishment and elation on their faces.

I didn't even realize that the "crossover" step they'd shaped in my second lesson had cured my childhood balance problems, until I found myself, during the free-skating period after class, sailing around corners blithely on my outside edges. And more! By the third lesson I could do spins, real spins like the skaters on TV, and natty little jump turns I never dreamed of aspiring to in childhood (these were at first shaped most ingeniously along the wall). What a revelation. The difficulty in learning such skills is caused not by physical requirements but by the absence of good shaping procedures.

Skiing is another example. The advent of the Fiberglas ski and ski boot has made skiing possible for the multitudes, not just for the exceptionally athletic. But what gets the multitudes out on the slopes is the teaching methods that use short skis at first and shape each needed behavior (slowing down, turning, and stopping—and of course falling down and getting up) through a series of small, easily accomplished steps marked by positive reinforcement. I went to Aspen, took three skiing lessons, and skied down an entire mountain. The more vigorous in my beginners' class were tackling the intermediate slopes by the end of a week.

There have always been individual teachers who produce rapid results. I think what had changed in the last decade or two is that the principles which produce rapid results are becoming implicit in the standard teaching strategies: "This is the way to teach skiing; don't yell at them, follow steps one through ten, praise and reinforce accomplishment at each step, and you'll get most of them out on the slopes in three days." When most instructors are using shaping and reinforcement, and consequently getting rapid results, the rest find they have to shift to the new methods just to compete for jobs. If this is happening in every individual sport, it is probably a major contribution to the so-called fitness craze. Learning active skills has become fun.

Reinforcement in Business

In our country, labor and management traditionally adopt an adversary position. The idea that everyone is in the same game together has never been particularly popular in American business. General business practice seems to decree that each side try to get as much as possible from the other while giving as little as possible. Of course this is really dumb from a training standpoint, and some managements lean toward other approaches. In the sixties "sensitivity training" and other social-psychology approaches were popular, to enlighten management about the needs and feelings of co-workers and employees. One can be as enlightened as possible, however, and still not know what to do about an employee problem. The facts of business are that some people have more status and some less, some take orders and some give them. In our country, a working situation is, for the most part, *not* like a family, nor should it be. Family-type interpersonal problem solving is therefore inappropriate.

I was interested recently to see, cropping up here and there in business news and publications, a more trainerly approach—ways to use reinforcement that range from the ingenious to the downright brilliant. For example, one management consultant suggests that when part of a group must be laid off, you identify the bottom 10 percent and the top 20 percent. You lay off the poorest performers, but you also make sure to tell the top 20 percent that they are being retained because they're doing such a good job. What a sensible idea. Besides saving your best people some sleepless nights and reinforcing them quite powerfully under the worrisome circumstances, you may be motivating intermediate performers either to seek the reinforcement they can now see is available or to avoid falling into the lowest percentile themselves.

Reinforcements for middle-level, middle-aged managers can consist of more interesting work at their present level instead of offering hope of promotion, which they may not be able to handle (or may not want, if it involves relocating the family). Cash bonuses for nonsmokers and for quitting smoking are paid by one computer-software company, and for good reason: The products it makes can be damaged by smoke particles. Other reinforcements in widening use include free choice of working hours, the so-called "flextime" system (especially desirable for working mothers), working in self-managed production teams, and being rewarded for getting the job done rather than for putting in the hours. All of these management techniques are designed around what the worker actually finds reinforcing—what works for people, not just for profits.

Programs aimed at cost cutting and work speedups— programs that essentially try to force workers to do not *quite* as bad a job as they are presently doing—are not nearly as effective as programs that help workers to do a better job and then reward them for it. Corporations that use positive reinforcement often see the results on their bottom line. One splendid example is Delta Airlines, which is well known for taking very good care of its employees. During the 1981 recession, in spite of operating losses, Delta refused to lay off any of its 37,000 employees. In fact, it gave a company-wide 8 percent pay raise. In a long-established climate of positive reinforcement, the employees thought in the same terms; they turned around and reinforced the company by pooling funds and buying it a new airplane, a $30 million Boeing 767.

Reinforcement in the Animal World

Throughout this book I have spoken of the way reinforcement theory has enabled professional animal trainers to establish behaviors in creatures that simply cannot be trained by force: cats, cougars, chickens, birds in the air, bulls in china shops. Training with reinforcement has opened up areas of discovery that I believe we've only begun to explore in developing useful working partnerships with new, undomesticated species. It enables animals to show us abilities we otherwise might never know they had.

The U.S. Navy has been in the forefront in developing new uses for nondomestic animals, ranging from dolphin harbor patrols to pilot whale salvage locators. At a California test range, in water too deep, muddy, and cold for human divers, the U.S. Navy routinely uses trainer–sea lion teams to mark and recover spent missiles. Navy scientist Jim Simmons has experimented with pigeons as spotters in air-sea rescue operations. The pigeons, carried in light planes, are trained to peck a button if they see a yellow, orange, or red object (the colors of life jackets and life rafts). So far the eyesight and efficiency of the pigeons has vastly exceeded that of trained human spotters, especially over rough seas. Both the Coast Guard and the U.S. Air Force are presently field-testing the pigeon-powered Project Sea Hunt. As one Coast Guard commander put it, "Where else can I get experienced, highly qualified searchers who will literally work for chicken feed?"

Dr. M. J. Willard, a student of Skinner's, has developed systems for training small monkeys to be helping hands for quadriplegics. Controlled with vocal commands and trained with positive and negative reinforcements, the monkeys can operate light switches, change TV channels, turn pages, fetch specific items, load and unload a cassette player, and even spoon-feed the human patient. They are housebroken, are active all day, and can put themselves to bed at night. The monkeys' obligingness, unlike that, say, of Seeing Eye dogs, does not depend on generations of breeding for eagerness to please but on the efficacy of training with reinforcement. (Real affection and trust, however, can develop between the patient and the simian nurse.) I do not think we can even guess, at this point, what other animals and skills may be brought into our partnership in the next decades.

One of the advantages of reinforcement training is that you don't have to think up something for the animal to do and then train it to do that; you can reinforce anything the animal happens to offer and see where it leads. No one dreamed that harbor seals could "talk," but at the New England Aquarium trainers noticed that a rescued harbor seal, Hoover, seemed to be mimicking sounds. Mimicking human sounds was shaped by reinforcement, and soon Hoover was "saying" a number of things.

"Say hello to the lady, Hoover."

Hoover (in a guttural bass voice but very distinctly): "Hiya, honey, h'are yuh."

It's funny to hear, but also of real scientific interest to mammalogists and bioacousticians.

To me as a behavioral biologist the most useful and wonderful aspect of reinforcement training is the window that the training opens up into the animal's mind. It's been fashionable for decades to deny that animals have minds or feelings, and this was probably healthy—it cleared up a lot of superstitions, overinterpretation ("My dog understands every word I say"), and misreading. But then along came the ethologists, spearheaded by Konrad Lorenz, to point out that animals have internal states—anger, fear, and so on—and that these are signaled by very clearcut postures, expressions, and movements, which can be recognized and interpreted.

When you can see the subject and the subject can see

you, and yet both of you are protected from any physical encounter or bodily harm (perhaps the animal is inside a cage or pen and you are not), then the animal is free to express any internal states the training interaction provokes. Very often the animal begins directing the resulting social behavior at the trainer—in signals ranging from greeting behavior to temper tantrums. Knowing nothing about a particular species but knowing how any subject tends to react to various training events, one can learn more about the nature of a species' social signals in a half hour of training than in a month of watching the animal interact with its own kind. For example, if I see a dolphin jump up in the air and come down with a big splash in a pool of other dolphins, I can only speculate as to why it did that; but if, in a training session, I fail to reinforce something I had previously reinforced every time, and the dolphin jumps up in the air and comes down with a big, directed splash that soaks me from head to toe, I can say with some certainty that at least part of the time it would seem likely that jump-splashes are aggressive displays . . . and effective ones, too.

One can tell more than that. Engaging a wild animal in some simple shaping procedure can give you a startling glimpse of what might be called species temperament—of how not only that individual but that species tends to tackle the challenges in its environment. Teaching training to my class of keepers at the National Zoo, I used a number of different species as demonstration animals. I stood on my side of the fence, using a whistle as conditioned reinforcer, and tossing in food; the animals moved about freely on their side. The polar bears turned out to be immensely persistent and dogged. One bear which accidentally got reinforced while sitting still took to offering "sitting still" as a response; slavering hopefully, eyes glued to the trainer, it could sit still for half an hour or more, hoping for reinforcement. It seems possible that in an animal which stalks seals on ice floes for a living, this kind of tenacity and patience has important survival value.

I wouldn't have dreamed of going inside the elephant pens at the National Zoo, no matter how docilely the elephants obeyed their regular handlers. But with the help of keeper Jim Jones I did run a couple of "freestyle" training sessions through the bars with a young Indian female named Shanti. I decided to shape her to throw a Frisbee, starting with retrieving it. Shanti immediately started playing 101 Things to Do with a Frisbee, especially making noise (Jim told me elephants like to make noise). Shanti made noise with the Frisbee by holding it in her trunk and banging it on the wall, by rattling it along the bars like a child with a stick, or by putting it on the floor and shuffling it back and forth with her foot. I was already amused. Shanti was fun. She quickly learned to fetch the Frisbee to me in return for a toot on the whistle and snack from the bucket. She also quickly learned to stand just a *little* bit farther away each time so I had to reach farther in for the Frisbee. When I didn't fall for that, she whopped me on the arm. When Jim and I both yelled at her for that (a negative reinforcement of disapproval, which elephants respect), she started fetching nicely but pretended she'd forgotten how to pick up carrots. It took her a full minute, feeling the carrot in my hand with her trunk, while looking meaningfully into my bucket, to get me to understand that she preferred the apples and sweet potatoes that were also in there. When I proved to be intelligent and biddable in this matter, and started giving her the preferred reinforcements, she immediately used the same technique—feeling with the trunk tip while making meaningful glances and eye contact—to try to get me to open the padlock on her cage. Elephants are not just a little bit smart; elephants are eerily smart.

Species temperament shows up in many, many species in a shaping session. When I inadvertently failed to reinforce a hyena, instead of getting mad or quitting it turned on the charm, sitting down in front of me, grinning and chuckling like a fur-covered Johnny Carson. In shaping a wolf to go around a bush in its yard I made the same mistake, failing to reinforce it when I should have; the wolf looked over its shoulder, made eye contact with a long, thoughtful stare, then ran on, right round the bush, earning all the kibble I had in my pocket; it had sized up the situation, perhaps deciding that I was still in the game since I was still watching, and it had taken a chance and guessed at what would work. Big risk takers, wolves. If hyenas are comedians, wolves are Vikings.

Sometimes the animals understand reinforcement perfectly. Melanie Bond, in charge of the National Zoo's great apes, had started reinforcing Ham, the chimpanzee, for various behaviors. One morning he was accumulating his food rather than eating it, with the intention, Melanie supposed, of eating outdoors. When Ham saw that at last Melanie was going over to open the door and let him outside, he knew what to do: He handed her a stalk of celery.

I can sympathize with biologists who want to observe the natural behavior of animals without disturbing or interfering with that behavior in any way, and who thus reject gross interference such as training. And I can understand, though I do not sympathize with, the experimental psychologist who shuns any assumptions about animals that are purely observational and cannot be backed up by numerical data. But I remain convinced that shaping sessions offer a fruitful way to combine both approaches and that both field and laboratory workers who can't or don't consider this tool may be missing a bet.

Shaping and reinforcement, deftly used, may also be of enormous importance in gaining insight into otherwise impenetrable human minds. My friend Beverly worked as a therapist in an institution for multiply handicapped children—children both deaf and blind or paralyzed and retarded. She constructed a device that made patterns of colored lights in response to sounds made into a microphone. Debbie, a paralyzed and retarded victim of cerebral palsy, who lay listless and motionless in bed day and night, laughed when she first saw the lights. She heard her voice amplified, saw the lights increase, and immediately learned that she could make the lights dance herself by continuing to laugh and vocalize. This discovery, that she, Debbie, could cause an interesting event to happen, made it possible for the therapist to begin to teach Debbie to communicate. Another child, born with part of his skull missing and forced to wear a helmet at all times, had always been assumed to be totally blind, since he felt his way from spot to spot and failed to respond to any visual stimuli. Beverly was encouraging him to vocalize into her microphone for the reinforcement of hearing his own voice amplified. Then she realized the boy was orienting to the flickering colored lights too—and vocalizing longer and longer to make the colors dance. He could see just fine. Once the staff knew that, they had a whole new "channel" through which this child might be reached and helped.

In an institutional setting, this particular training toy ended up in a closet. Beverly had only a master's degree and was not expected to initiate innovative therapy. There were no research papers proving that the multiply handicapped could be helped with colored lights, and indeed the departure from established protocol was resented by other staff members. That is not the point. The point is that reinforcement training can provide a lot of illumination—not only to the subject but about the subject—and sometimes in just a few moments of training time.

Reinforcement and Society

It sometimes seems as if the behaviorists are preaching that everything in human behavior is a product of learning and conditioning, and that every human ill, from wars to warts, can be cured with proper use of reinforcement. This is, of course, not so. Behavior is a rich soup of external and internal responses, learned and unlearned. Individuality is inborn, as every mother knows (the biologist T. C. Schneirla demonstrated individual behavior even in insects). Furthermore, a tremendous amount of what

169

we do and feel is a product of our evolution as social animals. This includes our tendencies to cooperate and be good to each other ("reciprocal altruism") as well as our tendencies to react aggressively if someone tromps on our ideas or property ("territoriality"). And then what one does or says at a given moment may depend just as much on one's physical state as on past experience or future expectations: A person who is extremely hungry or has a bad cold may behave quite differently from the same person when comfortable, regardless of what else is going on.

So reinforcement has limitations, and I see nothing wrong with that. I envision our understanding of behavior as resembling three interlocking rings, like the Ballantine beer logo. In one ring are the behaviorists such as Skinner and everything we know about learning and cognition; in another ring are the ethologists such as Lorenz and everything we know about the biological evolution of behavior; and in the third ring is behavior we don't yet understand well, such as play. And each ring shares part of its contents by overlapping with the other two.

Since society does not consist entirely of exchanges of reinforcement, social experiments involving reinforcement in group settings have produced mixed results. For example, the use of reinforcement in a structured society—a prison, hospital, or detention home, say—may be undermined by the very people doing the reinforcing. A psychologist friend has described to me a token reinforcement system with juvenile offenders in detention that worked wonderfully in a pilot project but fell apart completely, even producing dissension and rebellion, when established at another institution. It turned out the people in charge were distributing reinforcements as instructed for classroom attendance and other desirable behavior, but they didn't smile when they handed out the tokens. And with that small lapse, which was regarded (and rightly, I think) as an insult by the macho young offenders, the whole effort crumbled.

Reinforcement has been used on an individual and group basis to foster not just specific behavior but characteristics of value to society—say, a sense of responsibility. Characteristics usually considered to be "innate" can also be shaped. You can, for example, reinforce creativity. My son Michael, while going to art school and living in a loft in Manhattan, acquired a kitten off the streets and reinforced it for "cuteness," for anything it did that amused him. I don't know how the cat defined that, but it became a most unusual cat—bold, attentive, loyal, and full of delightful surprises well into middle age. At Sea Life Park we shaped creativity with two dolphins—in an experiment that has now been much anthologized—by reinforcing anything the animals did that was novel and had not been reinforced before. Soon the subjects caught on and began "inventing" often quite amusing behaviors. One came up with wackier stuff than the other; on the whole, even in animals, degrees of creativity or imaginativeness can be innate. But training "shifts" the curve for everyone, so that *anyone* can increase creativity from whatever baseline he or she began at.

Society, especially in the school system, is sometimes criticized for dampening creativity rather than encouraging it. I think that while such criticism is warranted, it's understandable that society would prefer the status quo. Once those dolphins learned the value of innovating, they became real nuisances, opening gates, stealing props, and inventing mischief. Innovative people are unpredictable by definition, and perhaps society can stand only a certain percentage of these types. If everybody behaved like our creative dolphins, we'd never get anything done. So, very often, individual creativity is discouraged in favor of group norms. Perhaps the courage it takes to defy that trend benefits the innovators who do succeed.

I think the important impact of reinforcement theory on our society will be not to change specific behaviors or institutions but in the effect on individuals of positive reinforcement itself. Reinforcement is information—it's information about what you are doing that is *working*. If we have information about how to get the environment to reinforce us, then we control our environment; we are no longer at its mercy. Indeed, our evolutionary fitness to some extent depends on such success.

So subjects like to learn through reinforcement not for the obvious reason—to get food or other rewards—but because they actually get some control over what is happening. And the reason people like to modify the behavior of others through reinforcement is that the response is so gratifying. Seeing animals brighten up, little kids' eyes shine, people bloom and glow with accomplishment you have helped them achieve is in itself an extremely powerful reinforcement. One gets absolutely hooked on the experience of getting good results.

A curious but important corollary to training by reinforcement is that it breeds affection in both subject and trainer. When I was at Sea Life Park it happened several times that an untamed dolphin, having been shaped with food reinforcement, suddenly became quite docile, allowed itself to be petted, and solicited social attention without any effort by us to "hand-tame" it or train it to do so. I have seen this happen with horses too, sometimes in a single training session, and even with several species of zoo animals that were in no way gentled or made pets of. The animals behave as if they love the trainer.

The trainer rapidly develops an attachment, too. I remember Shanti the elephant and that wolf, D'Artagnan, with respect, and I even have a soft spot for that dunderheaded polar bear. What happens, I believe, is that the success of the training interchange tends to turn the participants into generalized conditioned reinforcers for each other. The trainer is the source of interesting, exciting, rewarding, life-enhancing events for the subject, and the subject's responses are interesting and rewarding for the trainer, so that they really do become attached. Not dependent, just attached. Comrades in the battle of life.

On the level of human interaction, good use of positive reinforcement can have profound effects. It develops and intensifies family feelings, cements friendships, gives children courage, and teaches them to be imaginative and skilled reinforcers in turn. It makes for great sex, for sex, after all, is in part a mutual exchange of positive reinforcements. If two people get really good at reinforcing each other, they are likely to be a happy pair.

Good use of reinforcement does not mean just scattering rewards around indiscriminately or never saying no. People do fall into that misconception. Once, watching a mother pushing a toddler in a stroller down the street, I noticed that every time the baby began to fret the mother stopped, got out a little bag of healthful snacks—raisins and nuts—and fed the child, although the child did not appear particularly hungry and sometimes pushed her hand away. Trying to do the right thing, she was conscientiously offering reinforcement to the child for fussing. She was also failing to check for rumpled clothes or other discomforts that might have been making the baby fuss in the first place.

None of us will ever be perfect, and I am not proposing that we should be thinking about reinforcements all the time. I am suggesting that a shift to using positive responses in interactions with others instead of the harshness, argumentativeness, and withdrawal that are the style in many households and organizations affects not only the individuals involved but, rippling outward, their whole portion of society.

It seems to me that American society is, for all its freedom, a punitive society. We carry a burden of Calvinistic negativeness that colors all our institutions and much of our judgment, no matter what our personal backgrounds. A switch to positive reinforcement can be a startling event. In 1981, a little town in Arizona, desperate to hang on to its good schoolteachers, set up a foundation, raised money locally, and gave cash bonuses to five teachers, selected by faculty and community vote, amounting in some cases to a month's salary. The money was presented at high school graduation, and the teachers got a spontaneous standing ovation from the students too. By the third year of operation the program seemed to be benefiting students as well as teachers. A typical mixed bag of races, ethnic backgrounds, and rich and poor, the students were by then ranking well above average on national testings.

What I sense as significant in this story is not the method of reinforcing the top teachers, a good idea in itself, but the fact that the event made the wire services and was national news. Switching to positive reinforcement is at this moment in our culture a novel idea. But then, quickly becoming an acceptable idea, it is no longer regarded as experimental or crackpot. One suspects that the news next year will be that other towns have followed suit.

It may take a generation or two, or three. I suspect that positive reinforcement—because it is now coupled with a body of theory that makes it possible to analyze what happens when things go wrong—is an idea that will over time prove to be too infectious to keep down. Most behaviorists would, I expect, agree with me, wondering only why it's taking so long.

Perhaps what the humanists object to most in behaviorism is the implication that everything in society could and should be run by reinforcement (as much of it is already—but badly run). I think this is a baseless fear. Skinner's imaginary society, Walden Two, set up entirely on patterns of reinforcement, would not, in my opinion as a biologist, work out. Idealistic societies, in imagination or in practice, sometimes fail to take into account or seek to eliminate such biological facts as status conflict. We are social animals after all, and as such we must establish dominance hierarchies. Competition within groups for increased status—in *all* channels, not just approved or ordained channels—is absolutely inevitable and in fact performs an important social function: Whether in utopias or herds of horses, the existence of a fully worked-out hierarchy operates to reduce conflict. You know where you stand, so you don't have to keep growling to prove it. I feel that individual and group status, and many other human needs and tendencies, are too complex to be either met or overridden by planned arrangements of reinforcement, at least on a long-term basis.

What bothers the behaviorists, in turn, is their recognition of the many situations in society where proper use of reinforcement could be effective and where we stubbornly, stupidly, unceasingly prefer to do it wrong. For instance: giving arms and aid to countries we *hope* will regard us favorably. Come on! Rewarding someone else in hope of gain to oneself doesn't work; it backfires even on the simplest level ("She only invited me to her party so I'd bring a present; I hate her." "Aunt Tilly's being extraordinarily nice today; wonder what the old bat wants *this* time"). I'm also not sure that our being tough on countries that misbehave is any better. What if they don't care? What if they wanted to get us mad in the first place?

I realize this may be simplistic, but I also think it is simpleminded to go on and *on* behaving as a nation in ways that any rat reinforcer can tell you are guaranteed not to work. As a nation, as well as on an individual level, we ought to be continuously asking ourselves the trainer's fundamental question: What am I actually reinforcing?

The laws of reinforcement are powerful tools. But the rule book is far more versatile than some people have supposed, in fact more versatile than some people would like it to be. To be using reinforcement is to be involved in a process of continual change, of continual give-and-take, of continual growth. One becomes aware of the dualistic, two-way nature of this communion. One becomes more aware of others and, inevitably, more aware of oneself. It could be said that training is a process that requires one to be both inside and outside of one's own skin at the same time. Who is the trainer and who is the trained? Both change and both learn.

Some people have seen reinforcement theory as a method of control, of manipulation, of restriction of individuals and society. But societal changes must begin with personal changes—with shifts in what benefits the individual—just as species changes must begin in the individual gene. Social change cannot be dictated from above—at least not for long (Orwell's *1984* is wrong, biologically). Living creatures have a right not only to food and shelter but to a reinforcing environment. The use and understanding of reinforcement is an individual experience, which may lead to benefits for all. Far from being constricting, it frees each one of us to experience, be aware of, and enhance not the mechanistic aspects of living but the rich and wonderful diversity of all behavior.

Index

ABOUT THE AUTHOR

KAREN PRYOR pursues two careers, as a scientist and as a writer. Educated at Cornell University, with graduate work in zoology at the University of Hawaii, New York University, and Rutgers, she was a founder of Hawaii's Sea Life Park and Oceanic Institute, where her work with porpoises established her as an authority on learning and training as well as on marine-mammal behavior. She has lectured widely on her research to both lay and scientific audiences, and serves as a consultant to several government agencies and to private industry. Her first book, *Nursing Your Baby*, has sold more than two million copies. She is a contributor to *New York* magazine, *Psychology Today*, *Omni*, *Reader's Digest*, and other periodicals. She is also the author of two books on dolphin training and behavior, *Lads Before the Wind: Diary of a Dolphin Trainer*, and *Dolphin Societies: Discoveries and Puzzles*, with Kenneth S. Norris. The mother of three grown children, Ted, Michael, and Gayle Pryor, she is married to Jon Lindbergh and lives in the foothills of the Cascade Mountains in the state of Washington.